D1273087

Books by P. G. Wodehouse

BERTIE WOOSTER SEES IT THROUGH
THE RETURN OF JEEVES
PIGS HAVE WINGS
ANGEL CAKE
THE OLD RELIABLE
NOTHING SERIOUS
THE MATING SEASON
UNCLE DYNAMITE
SPRING FEVER
FULL MOON
JOY IN THE MORNING
MONEY IN THE BANK
QUICK SERVICE
EGGS, BEANS AND CRUMPETS
UNCLE FRED IN THE SPRINGTIME
THE CODE OF THE WOOSTERS
SUMMER MOONSHINE
THE CRIME WAVE AT BLANDINGS
LAUGHING GAS
YOUNG MEN IN SPATS
THE LUCK OF THE BODKINS
BLANDINGS CASTLE
BRINKLEY MANOR
THANK YOU, JEEVES
HEAVY WEATHER
MULLINER NIGHTS
HOT WATER
IF I WERE YOU!
BIG MONEY
VERY GOOD, JEEVES
SUMMER LIGHTNING
MR. MULLINER SPEAKING
MONEY FOR NOTHING
MEET MR. MULLINER
BILL THE CONQUEROR
SAM IN THE SUBURBS
THE SMALL BACHELOR
CARRY ON, JEEVES
DIVOTS
HE RATHER ENJOYED IT
LEAVE IT TO PSMITH
JEEVES
WHITE HOPE
GOLF WITHOUT TEARS
MOSTLY SALLY
THREE MEN AND A MAID
THE LITTLE WARRIOR
INDISCRETIONS OF ARCHIE
LOVE AMONG THE CHICKENS
THE INTRUSIONS OF JIMMY
THE PRINCE AND BETTY
SOMETHING NEW
UNEASY MONEY
THE LITTLE NUGGET
A GENTLEMAN OF LEISURE
A DAMSEL IN DISTRESS
PICCADILLY JIM

Collections

NOTHING BUT WODEHOUSE
WODEHOUSE ON GOLF
THE WEEKEND WODEHOUSE

P. G. WODEHOUSE

America, I like you

ILLUSTRATIONS BY MARC SIMONT

1956
SIMON AND SCHUSTER, NEW YORK

PUBLISHED BY SIMON AND SCHUSTER, INC.
ROCKEFELLER CENTER, 630 FIFTH AVENUE
NEW YORK 20, N. Y.
FIRST PRINTING
LIBRARY OF CONGRESS CATALOG CARD NUMBER: 56-7486
MANUFACTURED IN THE UNITED STATES OF AMERICA
AMERICAN BOOK–STRATFORD PRESS, NEW YORK

Contents

America,
I like you

Thanks for the Memory, Such As It Is

1

WHEN I ANNOUNCE that I was born in England and reveal that I am an author, you will probably give a start of surprise and a puzzled look will come into your faces.

"But why," you will say, "are you writing this thing, whatever it is, in book form and not dishing it out on one of those lecture tours to which British authors are so addicted?"

You have touched on my secret sorrow. Nothing would please me better than to be out and about, rolling vast audiences in the aisles and having ladies' clubs tearing up the seats, but it is beyond my scope. I am not a convincing talker. Very few of the island race are, and this sometimes leads to unfortunate results. As witness the story of the two English explorers.

These two explorers—one from The Grange, Lower-Smattering-on-the-Wissel, Worcestershire, the other from Meadowsweet Hall, Higgleford-cum-Wortlebury-beneath-the-Hill, Hants—were exploring in South America and chanced to meet one morning on a narrow mountain ledge high up in the Andes where there was not space for either of them to pass. It was a situation fraught with embarrassment, and for perhaps an hour they stood gazing at each other in silence. Then it occurred to one of them that by leaping outward and putting a bit of spin on himself he could jump around the other. This he proceeded to do, but by the worst of luck the same thought had occurred simultaneously to the second explorer, with the result that they collided in mid-air and perished in the fall from the precipice.

This would not have happened if they had been convincing talkers.

I have always had only the most rudimentary gift of speech. I was reading a book the other day entitled *How to Become a Charming Conversationalist*, and it took all the heart out of me.

"Are you audible?" it asked me. "Are you clear? Pleasant? Flexible? Vigorous? Well modulated? Acceptable in pronunciation? Agreeable in laughter?" And the answer was No. I was husky, hoarse, muffled, thin, indistinct, glottal, monotonous, jumbled, unacceptable in pronunciation and disagreeable in laughter—in short, the very opposite of Thomas Lomonaco, the courteous and popular Brooklyn taxi driver who was driving his taxi one afternoon not long ago at Jamaica Avenue and Seventy-fifth Street when he was hailed by Elmer Hinitz.

"Gimme about fifty cents' worth," said Elmer Hinitz.

At Eightieth Street he produced a switch knife and, leaning forward, tapped Thomas Lomonaco on the shoulder.

"This is a stick-up," he announced.

"No. Really?" said Mr. Lomonaco, interested.

"Yah. Slip me your money or I will expunge you."

"I see your point," said Mr. Lomonaco, "and I can fully appreciate your desire to add to your savings, with times as hard as they are in this disturbed postwar era. But your whole plan of campaign is rendered null and void by the fact that I have no money. Would it soften your disappointment if I offered you one of my cigarettes? They are mild. They satisfy."

Mr. Hinitz accepted a cigarette and the conversation proceeded along pleasant lines as far as 118th Street and Jamaica Avenue, when Mr. Lomonaco said, "Say, look. Do you know the police station?"

Mr. Hinitz said he did not.

"Most picturesque," said Mr. Lomonaco. "You'll like it. Let's drive there."

And his talk was so convincing that Mr. Hinitz immediately agreed. A good idea, he said, and he is now in custody, held in $1,000 bail.

To reporters Mr. Lomonaco stated that this was the second time he had been stuck up while pursuing his profession. The other time was in Williamsburg, where a passenger threatened him with a pistol. Mr. Lomonaco, says the daily paper to which I subscribe, "talked him out of the pistol." Obviously a man who must have spent months, if not years, standing in front of a mirror, stretching his muscles, raising himself on tiptoe, rolling the head from side to side and repeating a hundred times the words "Give me a box of mixed biscuits, a mixed biscuit box, and sell me some short silk socks and shimmering satin sashes."

For this—in addition to lying on your back with a heavy weight on your stomach and shouting "Li-yah! Li-yah!"—is apparently what you have to do to become a convincing talker, and I can't manage it. It would cut into my time too much. So, as I said before, that is why I am writing this book and not delivering it verbally to lecture audiences.

As to what the book is, there will no doubt be fierce controversy. You can't call it an autobiography exactly; the word is too important. Another reason why its claim to be ranked as an autobiography falls to the ground and fails to hold water is that in order to write an autobiography that really is an autobiography you need a good memory, and mine is more like a sieve than anything human. On several occasions it has been suggested to me that I might take a pop at this sort of thing. "Yours has been a long life, Wodehouse," people say. "You look about a hundred and four. What memories you must have!" And it makes me feel silly to have to reply, "Memories? Ah, yes, to be sure. The only trouble is that I'm darned if I can remember them." I am absolutely incapable of filling a hundred pages with

CHAPTER ONE: The Infant
CHAPTER TWO: Childhood Days
CHAPTER THREE: Adolescence

and so forth. All I can recollect of my childhood days is that I used to play with an orange, which is not good for more than a paragraph, and that at the age of six I read the whole of Pope's *Iliad,* which naturally nobody is going to believe. And as for adolescence, I recall nothing except that I had a lot of pimples. (Today I have none. How often that happens! We start out in life with more pimples than we know what to do with and, in the careless arrogance of youth, fancy that they are going to last forever; but one morning we find that we are down to our last half dozen, and then those go. There is a lesson in this for all of us, I think.)

I suppose what I ought to have done would have been to take some sort of memory-training course. English literature is full of tips on how to train the memory. Guiliemus Groterolus Bergomatis (1565) advises washing the feet in warm water. He also says, "The braynes of a henne doth helpe the memorie," which is not much good to us, for when did anyone ever meet a hen that had any brains, and warns us against "garlyke, leekes, onyions, also peason and moyste brothes." (Odd how this comic spelling has so completely gone out nowadays. In 1565 it used to have them in stitches.)

William Vaughan (1600) recommends the bathing of the head four times a year with hot lye made of ashes, followed by a cold shower. "The sodaine powring down of cold water . . ." No, please, William. If you mean "sudden pouring," say "sudden pouring." A man of your stature has no need to descend to clowning for the sake of a cheap laugh. "The sodaine powring down of cold water," he says, "is very goode, for thereby the natural heate is stirred within the bodie and the memorie is quickened."

But you remember the cold shower. That is the catch.

On the whole, the simplest memory-training methods are probably the best. A member of the British Parliament was once standing in the lobby of the House when a tall, distinguished-looking old gentleman came up and begged for a moment of his time.

"I have heard of you as one who takes up unpopular causes," he said, "and I should be extremely grateful if you would listen to my story."

It was a sad story. By industry and thrift he had amassed a large fortune, and now his relatives had robbed him of it and, not content with that, had placed him in a mental home. This was his day out.

"I have put the facts down in this document," he concluded. "Study it at your leisure. Communicate with me at your leisure. Thank you, sir, thank you. Good day."

Much moved by the other's exquisite courtesy, the M.P. took the paper, shook hands, promised that he would do everything in his power and turned to go back to the debate. As he did so, he received a kick in the seat of the pants which nearly sent his spine shooting through his hat.

"Don't forget!" said the old gentleman.

2

I don't think, though, that even if my memory were like a steel trap I would ever have the nerve to attempt a full-dress autobiography. To do that, you have to be somebody in the big league, one of those who have done the world's work, like Polly Adler, and I—let's face it—am a pretty insignificant sort of blister, not at all the type that leaves footprints on the sands of time, as the fellow said. Ask the first ten men you meet "Have you ever heard of P. G. Wodehouse?" and nine of them will answer No. The tenth, being hard of hearing, will say "Down the passage, first door on the right."

Not that I regret this obscurity. There are compensations for being just one of the *canaille*. People are always coming up to me in the street and saying "Hello there, Wodehouse. Don't you wish you were a celebrity?" And my invariable reply is "No, Smith or Stokes or Campanella" (if it happens to be Roy Campanella), "I do not."

Nothing would induce me to be a celebrity. I would as soon be someone for whom the police are spreading one of those dragnets. If in a weak moment you let yourself become a prominent figure in the public eye these days, you are nothing but a straight man for all the comedians in the country. Joshing the eminent is now a national sport.

It was not always so. There was a time when celebrities lived the life of Riley. Everyone looked up to them and respected them. They had never had it so good. And then suddenly everything changed. Out like a cloud of mosquitoes came a horde of bright young men with fountain pens and notebooks, dogging their footsteps and recording their every unguarded speech, till today you can tell a celebrity at a glance by the nervous way he keeps looking over his shoulder and jumping at sudden noises. Many of them get the illusion that they are being followed about by little men with black beards.

It was *The New Yorker* that started it all with its Profiles. It had the idea that if you tracked down your celebrity, lulled him into a false security with the respectfulness of your demeanor, got him talking and then went home and wrote a piece showing him up as a complete bird-brain, everybody—except the celebrity—would get a hearty laugh out of it. They "did" Ernest Hemingway a year or two ago, sending a female reporter to spend the afternoon with him and write down every word he uttered, with of course the jolliest results. If you write down every word uttered by anyone over a period of several hours you are bound to hook an occasional fatuous remark.

It is getting so nowadays that celebrities are scared of opening their mouths. And perhaps I am wrong in saying that this harrying of the famous is a new thing, for I have been reading a book by Harold Nicolson in which he tells how he felt as a young man when dining with Tennyson.

> An aching pause, and in a crisis of embarrassment one would pass into the dining room. The Laureate would begin to carve the boiled beef. A little fluttering conversation from Mrs. Tennyson about Yarmouth pier, a sudden growl from the Laureate—"I like my

> meat in wedges"—and the subject of Yarmouth pier would flutter down to another prolonged and awful silence.

One's sympathies are supposed, of course, to be with Harold. Mine are not. Tennyson is the one I am sorry for. The operative word in the passage I have quoted is the word "would." It shows us that the writer is not describing just one dinner at which he happened by bad luck to be present. He was always there. You couldn't keep him away. He oozed into the house like oil. Day after day the good gray poet—if he was a good gray poet, I can never remember which of them were—would be starting to dig in and get his, and he would look up and there would be Harold Nicolson, back again in the same old chair with the same popeyed expression on his face and his ears sticking up like a wire-haired terrier's. No wonder he went into a prolonged silence. It is a most unpleasant thing, when you want to be alone with your boiled beef, to look up from the carrots and gravy and see Harold Nicolson, knowing that he is just counting the minutes till you provide an amusing paragraph for his memoirs by saying something silly or choking on a hot potato.

To you young men of today—you revolting goggle-eyed young snoopers—I would say this: Lay off those celebrities. Stop chivvying them. Give the poor slobs a break. You may be celebrities yourselves at any moment, so remember the story of the mother who was walking with her child on

Hollywood Boulevard when a group of men in make-up came along.

The child pointed.

"Look, Mamma. Movie actors."

"Hush, dear," said the mother. "You don't know what *you* may come to some day."

And it is not as if the celebrities got anything out of it, though there have been indications recently that better times are coming. The name of John Harrington is probably not familiar to my readers, so I will explain that he is the director of sports at a Chicago broadcasting station, and the other day he received a stunning blow. He is still walking around in circles, kicking stones and muttering to himself, and the mildest of the things he mutters is "Bloodsuckers! Bloodsuckers!" If you care to describe him as cut to the quick, it will be all right with me.

What happened was that he wanted to interview some members of the Kansas City Athletics baseball club and was informed by them that they would be charmed if he would do so, provided he unbelted fifty dollars, cash in advance. No fifty fish, no interview. It was the first time anything like this had happened to him. One gets new experiences.

Hats off, I say, to those Kansas City athletes. For years there has been too much of this thing of notebooked young men sidling up to the celebrated and getting away with all sorts of good stuff without paying a cent for it. The celebs were supposed to be compensated by a few kind words chucked in at the beginning. "He looks like a debonair ma-

gician, quick and agile, in his fashionable suit of gray and elegant black patent leather slippers." That was what the London *Daily Express* said about Mr. Cecil Beaton not long ago when he gave them an interview. A poor substitute for hard cash.

And it was an important interview, too, for in it Mr. Beaton revealed for the first time the sensational facts in connection with his recent visit to an amusing chateau in the wine country of France.

"Summer had come," he said (exclusive), "and I found the atmosphere most stimulating. We had an amusing dish —a delightful creamy mixture of something I can't quite remember, but I recall a mountain of truffles in it."

All that free! The circulation of the *Express* doubled. Lord Beaverbrook was enabled to buy two more houses in Jamaica. But what did Mr. Beaton get out of it? Not a thing except the passing gratification of seeing himself described as a debonair magician in black patent leather slippers. Does that pay the rent? It does not. You can wear black patent leather slippers till your eyes bubble, but the landlord still wants his so much per each week. High time those Kansas City boys put their foot down.

Though they were not the first to do it. Apparently you have to be a baseball player to stand up for your rights. John Crosby was writing the other day about an exchange of views which took place some years ago between Bill Terry, at that time manager of the Giants, and a representative of *The New Yorker*, which wanted to do a Profile of him. (A *New Yorker* Profile takes up eighty-three pages in the middle of the magazine and goes on for months and months and months.)

"And where were you born, Mr. Terry?" inquired the Profile hound, starting to get down to it.

A wary look came into Wm.'s face.

"Young fella," he said, "that information will cost you a lot of money."

That ended the love feast. They had to fill up the eighty-three pages with one of those solid, thoughtful things of Edmund Wilson's.

Hats off, therefore, also to Bill Terry. But though I approve of this resolve on the part of the celebrated to get in on the ground floor and make a bit, I am not blind to the fact that there is a danger of the whole thing becoming more than a little sordid. At first, till a regular scale of prices is set up and agreed to by both contracting parties, one foresees a good deal of unpleasant wrangling.

Let us say that you are a young fellow named Spelvin who in a recent golf tournament lost forty-three balls on eighteen holes, beating the record set up in 1951 by Otis G. Follansbee of Westhampton Beach, New York. It will not be long before there is a ring at the bell, followed by the appearance of a gentleman of the press.

"Good morning, Mr. Spelvin."

"Good morning."

"I am from *Time*. Three and forty balls on a round of

golf last week we understand you lost and naturally anxious are our readers to hear——"

"How much?"

"Twenty dollars?"

"Make it thirty."

"Call it twenty-five. Okay?"

"Well, it depends. Are you going to refer to me as stumpy balding spectacled George Spelvin (28) no Hogan he?"

"Certainly not. I thought something on the lines of a debonair magician, quick and agile."

"Yes, I like that."

"Adding that not spoiled you has success."

"Excellent. I don't mind knocking off a couple of dollars for that."

"Make it five."

"No, not worth five."

"Very well. Now tell me, Mr. Spelvin, can you describe your feelings when your forty-third ball disappeared over the horizon?"

"I felt fine."

"And may I say you did it all for the wife and kiddies?"

"Not for twenty-five bucks you mayn't. We'd better go back to the thirty we were talking about."

You see what I mean. Sordid. These negotiations are better left to one's agent. I have instructed mine to arrange for a flat payment of fifteen dollars, to be upped, of course, if they want to know what I had for dinner at that amusing chateau in the wine country.

America, I Like You

The name of the *Time* man in the foregoing scene was not mentioned, but I presume he was one of those appearing in a little poem which I jotted down just now on the back of an old envelope after brooding, as I so often brood, on the list in *Time* of its editors, managing editors, assistant managing editors, deputy assistant managing editors, contributing editors, sympathetic encouraging editors, researchers and what not, which is my favorite reading. You will generally find me with my feet up on the mantelpiece, poring over this fascinating column, and it always inspires me to bigger and better things.

I must confess that often I'm
A prey to melancholy
Because I do not work on *Time*.
It must be jolly. Golly!
No other human bliss but pales
Beside the feeling that you're
One of nine hundred—is it?—males
And females of such stature.

How very much I would enjoy
To call Roy Alexander "Roy"
And have him say "Hello, my boy!"

Not to mention being on terms of easy
camaraderie with

Edward O. Cerf
Richard Oulahan Jr
Bernadine Beerheide

Thanks for the Memory, Such As It Is

Virginie Lindsley Bennett
Rodney Campbell
Estelle Dembeck
Dorothea L. Grine
Eldon Griffiths
Hillis Mills
Joseph Purtell
Old Uncle Fuerbringer and all.

Alas, I never learned the knack
(And on *Time*'s staff you need it)
Of writing English front to back
Till swims the mind to read it.
Tried often I've my darnedest, knows
Goodness, but with a shock I'd
Discover once again my prose
Had failed to go all cockeyed.

So though I wield a fluent pen,
There'll never be a moment when
I join that happy breed of men.

I allude to (among others)

Douglas Auchincloss
Lester Bernstein
Gilbert Cant
Edwin Copps
Henry Bradford Darrach Jr.
Barker T. Hartshorn
Roger S. Hewlett
Jonathan Norton Leonard

America, I Like You

F. Sydnor Trapnell
Danuta Reszke-Birk
Deirdre Mead Ryan
Yi Ying Sung
Content Peckham
Quinera Sarita King
Old Uncle Fuerbringer and all,
Old Uncle Fuerbringer and all.

A pity, but too late to alter it now.

3

Another thing about an autobiography is that, to attract the cash customers, it must be full of good stories about the famous, and I never can think of any. If it were just a matter of dropping names, I could do that with the best of them, but mere name-dropping is not enough. You have to have the sparkling anecdote as well, and any I could provide would be like the one Young Griffo, the boxer, told Hype Igoe about his meeting with Joe Gans, the then lightweight champion. Having just been matched to fight Gans, he was naturally anxious to get a look at him before the formal proceedings began, and here is how he told the dramatic tale of their encounter.

> I was goin' over to Philadelphia to see a fight, Hype, and my manager asks me would I like to meet Joe Gans. He asks me would I like to meet Joe Gans, Hype, and

Thanks for the Memory, Such As It Is

I said I would. So we arrive in Philadelphia and we start out for one of the big sporting places where the gang all held out, and my manager asks me again do I want to meet Joe Gans, and I say I do. So we go to this big sporting place, Hype, and there's a big crowd standing around one of the tables, and somebody asks me would I like to meet Joe Gans, he's over at that table, and I say I would. So he takes me to the table and says "Here's Young Griffo, Joe," he says. "He wants to meet you," he says. And sure enough it was Gans all right. He gets up from the table. "Hello, Griff," he says, and I say, "Hello, Joe."

This was all. You might have thought more was coming, but no. He had met Gans, Gans had met him. It was the end of the story. My autobiography would be full of stuff like that.

> I had long wished to make the acquaintance of Sir (then Mr.) Winston Churchill, but it was not till my third year in London that I was enabled to gratify this ambition. A friend took me to the House of Commons, and we were enjoying tea on the terrace when the object of my admiration came by.
>
> "Oh, Winston," said my friend, "I want you to meet Mr. Wodehouse."
>
> "How do you do?" said Mr. Churchill.
>
> "How do you do?" I replied.

You can't charge people five dollars or whatever it is for that sort of thing.

This, then, is nothing so ambitious as an autobiography. What I am about to relate is just the simple story of my love affair with the United States of America, starting when we were both fifty years younger in a strange city where Thirty-fourth Street was uptown and there was no Marilyn Monroe, no Liberace, no Zsa Zsa Gabor and only a rough preliminary scenario of Billy Rose, he being five years old at the time (and a sweet child, so they tell me). And we now approach the question of how—if at all—it is to be read, and I should like to make a suggestion with regard to the *modus operandi*, if that is the expression I want.

What I would wish the reader to do is to approach the thing in the indulgent spirit in which he listens to an after-dinner speech. Let him try to imagine that he is leaning back in his chair flushed with heady wines and smoking a good cigar and that I, up at the top table, am in the process of being reminded by a remark of the last speaker of a little story about two Irishmen which may be new to some of you present here tonight. It will make all the difference.

It would, indeed, be a good idea if you actually had a square meal before starting to tackle the book. My publishers will support me in this. Simon tells me that when he and Schuster received my manuscript the mere sight of it gave them both a sort of sinking feeling. They spent the day shoving it across the table at each other, each trying to avoid the task of reading it. Two editors named Schwed and Goodman were called in and told to have a go, but after a couple of pages both resigned and are now coffee-planting in Kenya. The situation began to look like a deadlock, and then suddenly the idea struck Schuster—or it may have been Simon—that things might brighten after they had had dinner.

They dined as follows:

Le Dîner

Caviar Frais

Consommé Brunoise aux Quenelles

Darne de Saumon au Beurre de Montpellier

Blanchailles

Caille Demidoff

Sylphides à la Crême d'Ecrevisses

Mousse de Jambon à la Neva

Pointes d'Asperges à la Tallulah Bankhead

Fraises Melba

Diablotins

Corbeille de Fruits Exotiques

and the result was magical. Full to the eyebrows, with the coffee and old brandy at their side, they felt equal to anything now, and they pitched in and were past page 100 before they knew where they were.

So if you are hesitating about reading any further, say to yourself, "Courage! It can be done," and stoke up and go to it.

A word about the title. It is taken (by kind permission) from that grand old song by the Messrs. Kalmar and Ruby, which runs:

Thanks for the Memory, Such As It Is

America, I like you!
You're like an uncle to me.
From mountain to mountain
To you my affection
Is touching each hemisphere.
Just like a little children
Climbing his father's lap,
America, how are you?
And there's a hundred people feeling the same.
The A stands for our Navy,
The M for the soldiers we've got,
The E for the heagle which flies up above us,
The R for we can't go wrong,
I for Independence,
C stands for brave and bold,
America, I like you,
Don't bite the hand that's feeding you.

For years this stirring ballad has been a household word from one end of the country to the other. Harry Ruby often sings it at parties in Beverly Hills. And very unpleasant it sounds, I am told, for his voice is breaking.

An Old Sweetheart Who Has Put on Weight

1

WHY AMERICA? I have often wondered about that. Why, I mean, from my earliest years, almost back to the time when I was playing with that orange, was it America that was always to me the land of romance? It is not as though I had been intoxicated by visions of cowboys and red Indians. Even as a child I never became really cowboy-conscious, and to red Indians I was definitely allergic. I wanted no piece of them.

And I had no affiliations with the country. My father had spent most of his life in Hong Kong. So had my Uncle Hugh.

And two other uncles had been known to the police of Calcutta and Singapore. You would have expected it to be the Orient that would have called to me. "Put me somewheres east of Suez," you would have pictured me saying to myself. But it didn't work out that way. People would see me walking around with a dreamy look in my eyes and my mouth hanging open as if I had adenoids and they would whisper to one another, "He's thinking of America." And they were right. I thought of America practically incessantly. I yearned for it with a fervor which equaled, if not surpassed, that of a Tin-Pan-Alley song writer longing to go back back back to his old Kentucky shack. But it was not till 1904—April 24, now a national holiday—that I was able at last to set foot on the sidewalks of New York.

On leaving school I had accepted employment in a London bank, and this restricted my freedom of movement. It was only after several years that I threw off the shackles and resigned.

Well, when I say "resigned . . ."

Let me tell you the story of the new ledger.

One of the things that sour authors, as every author knows, is being asked by people to write something clever in the front pages of their books. It was, I believe, George Eliot who in a moment of despondency made this rather bitter entry in her diary:

> Dear Diary: Am I a wreck tonight! I feel I never want to see another great admirer of my work again. It's

> not writing novels that's hard. I can write novels till the cows come home. What slays you is this gosh-darned autographing. "Oh, *please*! Not just your *name*. Won't you write something *clever*?" To hell with it.

And Richard Powell, the whodunit author, was complaining along similar lines in a recent issue of the *American Writer*. "I begin sweating," he said, "as soon as someone approaches me with a copy of one of my books."

I feel the same. When I write a book, the golden words come pouring out like syrup, but let a smiling woman steal up to me with my latest and ask me to jot down something clever on the front page, and it is as though some hidden hand had removed my brain and substituted for it an order of cauliflower. There may be men capable of producing something clever on the spur of the moment, but I am not of their number. I like at least a month's notice, and even then I don't guarantee anything.

The only time I ever wrote anything really clever on the front page of a book was when I was a wage slave in this bank of which I was speaking. I was in the Cash department at the time, and a new ledger came into the office and was placed in my charge. It had a white, gleaming front page, and suddenly, as I sat gazing at it, there floated into my mind like drifting thistledown the idea of writing on it a richly comic description of the celebrations and rejoicings marking the Formal Opening of the New Ledger.

It was great. But great. Though fifty-four years have

passed since that day, I can still remember that. There was a bit about my being presented to His Gracious Majesty the King (who, of course, attended the function) which makes me laugh even now. ("From his tie he took a diamond tie-pin, and smiled at me, and then he put it back.") But the whole thing was terrific. I can't give the details. You will have to take my word for it that it was one of the most screamingly funny things ever written. I sat back on my stool and felt like Shakespeare. I was all in a glow.

Then came the reaction. The Head Cashier was rather an austere man who on several occasions had expressed dissatisfaction with the young Wodehouse, and something seemed to whisper to me that, good as the stuff was, it would not go any too well with him. Briefly, I got cold feet and started to turn stones and explore avenues in the hope of finding some way of making everything pleasant for all concerned. In the end I decided that the best thing to do was to cut the page out with a sharp knife.

A few mornings later the stillness of the bank was shattered by a sudden yell of triumph, not unlike the cry of a Brazilian wildcat leaping on its prey. It was the Head Cashier discovering the absence of the page, and the reason he yelled triumphantly was that he was feuding with the stationers and for weeks had been trying to get the goods on them in some way. He was at the telephone in two strides, asking them if they called themselves stationers. I suppose they replied that they did, for he then touched off his bomb-

shell, accusing them of having delivered an imperfect ledger, a ledger with the front page missing.

This brought the head stationer around in person calling heaven to witness that when the book left his hands it had been all that a ledger should be, if not more so.

"Somebody must have cut out the page," he said.

"Absurd!" said the Head Cashier. "Nobody but an imbecile would cut out the front page of a ledger."

"Then," said the stationer, "you must have an imbecile in your department. Have you?"

The Head Cashier started. This opened up a new line of thought.

"Why, yes," he said, for he was a fair-minded man. "There is P. G. Wodehouse."

"Weak in the head is he, this Wodehouse?"

"Very, so I have always thought."

"Then have him on the carpet and question him narrowly," said the stationer.

This was done. They got me under the lights and grilled me, and I had to come clean. It was immediately after this that I found myself at liberty to embark on the life literary.

2

From my earliest years I had always wanted to be a writer. I started to write at the age of five. (What I was doing before that, I don't know. Just loafing, I suppose.)

It was not that I had any particular message for humanity. I am still plugging away and not a ghost of one so far, so it begins to look as though, unless I suddenly hit mid-season form, humanity will remain a message short. I just wanted to write, and was prepared to write anything that had a chance of getting into print.

Actually, I had made considerable progress while still working in the bank. I had had my setbacks, of course—the *English Illustrated Magazine* accepted a short story of mine and were going to pay me fifteen shillings for it, but after they had had it six months a new editor came in and returned the thing to me with a rejection slip—but I had received eleven shillings for an article in *Today* and half a crown for some verses in *Scraps*, so when I turned pro I was off, as you might say, to a running start. As I surveyed the literary scene, everything looked pretty smooth to me. My lodgings cost me a guinea a week, breakfast, lunch and dinner included, and it seemed absurd to suppose that a man of my gifts would not be able to earn a weekly twenty-one shillings, especially in the London market of that time.

The early years of the twentieth century in London—it was in 1902 that the Hong Kong and Shanghai Bank decided (and a very sensible decision, too) that the only way to keep solvent was to de-Wodehouse itself—were not too good for writers at the top of the tree, the big prices being still in the distant future, but they were fine for an industrious young fellow who asked no more than to pick up the occasional half-guinea. The dregs, of whom I was one, sat extremely pretty *circa* 1902. There were so many evening papers and weekly papers and monthly magazines that you were practically sure of landing your whimsical piece on The Language of Flowers or your parody of Omar Khayyám somewhere or other after about say thirty-five shots.

I left the bank at the beginning of September, and by the end of December I found that I had made £65 6.7, so for a beginner I was doing pretty well. But I was not saving enough for the visit to New York, on which my heart was set, and I saw where the trouble lay. I needed something in the way of a job with a regular salary.

There was an evening paper in London in those days called the *Globe*. It was a hundred and five years old and was printed—so help me—on pink paper. (One of the other evening papers was printed on green paper. Life was very full then, very rich.) It was a profitable source of income to all young writers because it ran on its front page what were called Turnovers, thousand-word articles of almost unparalleled dullness which turned over onto the second page. A guinea was the guerdon for these. You dug them out of reference books.

In addition to the Turnovers the *Globe* also carried on its front page a column, supposedly humorous, entitled "By the Way," and one day I learned that the man who wrote it had been a master at my old school. These things form a bond. I asked him to work me in as his understudy when he wanted a day off, and he very decently did so, and when he was offered a better job elsewhere, I was taken on permanently. Three guineas a week was the stipend—roughly fifteen dollars—and it was precisely what I needed. The work was over by noon, and I had all the rest of the day for freelancing. I began to save. By April 1904 I had sixty pounds stashed away and a trip to New York became a practical proposition.

The *Globe* gave its staff five weeks' holiday in the year. Eight days crossing the Atlantic and eight days crossing it back again was going to abbreviate my visit, but I should at least have nineteen days in Manhattan, so I booked my passage second class on the *St. Louis* and sailed on April 16. And on April 24 there I was.

Right from the start I don't think I ever had any doubts as to this being the New York of which I had heard so much. "It looks like New York," I said to myself as I emerged from the Customs sheds. "It smells like New York. Damme, it *is* New York." In which respect I differed completely from Signor Giuseppe Bertolo who, arriving there on the plane from Italy the other day, insisted against all argument that he was in San Francisco.

What he had overlooked was that to get from Italy to San Francisco you have to change at New York and take a westbound plane. All he knew was that his son in San Francisco had told him to come to Montgomery Street, where his—the son's—house was, so the moment the bus had deposited him at the terminus he hailed a taxi and gave the direction.

Now it so happens that there is a Montgomery Street in New York, down on the lower East Side, and the driver—José Navarro of 20 Avenue D, not that it matters—took him there. And this is where the plot begins to thicken. Nothing on Montgomery Street resembled the picture his son had sent him of the house for which he was headed, so Signor Bertolo decided to search on foot, and when he had not returned at the end of an hour Mr. Navarro drove to the Clinton Street police station and told his story. About 7 P.M. Signor Bertolo arrived at the police station, escorted by Patrolman Mario Pertini, and that was where things got complex and etched those deep lines which you can still see on the foreheads of the Clinton Street officials. For Signor Bertolo stoutly refused to believe that he was in New York. He insisted that he was in San Francisco. Hadn't he seen Montgomery Street with his own eyes? The fact that some men of ill-will had spirited away his son's house had, he said, nothing to do with the case.

After about forty minutes of this Police Lieutenant Daly drew Patrolman Pertini aside. There was a worried look on his face, and he was breathing rather stertorously.

"Look, Mario," he said. "Are you absolutely sure this *is* New York?"

"It's how I always heard the story, Lieut," said Patrolman Pertini.

"Have you any doubts?"

"If you had asked me that question an hour ago—nay, forty minutes ago—Lieut, I'd have said, 'No, none,' but now I'm beginning to wonder."

"Me, too. Tell me in your own words, Mario, what makes—or shall we say used to make you think this is New York."

"Well, I live in the Bronx. That's in New York."

"There may be a Bronx in San Francisco."

"And here's my badge. Lookut. See what it says on it. 'New York City.' "

"You can't go by badges. How do we know that some international gang did not steal your San Francisco badge and substitute this one?"

"Would an international gang do that?"

"You never can tell. They're always up to something," said Lieutenant Daly with a weary sigh.

Well, it all ended happily, I am glad to say. Somebody called up the Signor's son and put the Signor on the wire, and the son told him that New York really was New York and that he was to get on the westbound plane at once. And there he is now, plumb spang in Montgomery Street, San Francisco, and having a wonderful time. (He specifies this in a picture postcard to a friend in Italy, adding that he wishes he—the friend—were here.) It is a great weight off everybody's mind.

The whole episode recalls a picture in *Punch* fifty years ago of an English visitor to Paris leaning out of the window of the train at the Gare du Nord and saying to a porter, "*Quel est le nom de cette place?*"

Travelers to foreign parts should remember this. It is always safest to ask, "*Quel est le nom de cette place?*" before starting to explore.

3

To say that New York came up to its advance billing would be the baldest of understatements. Being there was like being in heaven without going to all the bother and expense of dying. And it is interesting—to me at any rate—to think that I saw more of New York in those nineteen days than in all the years I have spent there since. If you want to see a city, it is no good being a resident, you have to be a tourist. (Broadly speaking, a tourist is one who takes the sightseeing bus to Chinatown. I did this, and a friendly policeman showed me round. I tipped him a quarter. Well, how was I to know? In London its equivalent, a shilling, would have been lavish. I can still hear his indulgent laugh as he handed it back.)

What an amazingly attractive city New York was in those days! I still love it, of course, but today it is with the tempered affection which you feel for an old sweetheart who has put on a lot of weight. There is no concealing the fact that the dear old place has swollen visibly these last fifty years. In 1904, if I remember correctly, the tallest skyscraper was the New York *World* building. Handsome private houses lined Fifth Avenue. And the plays at the theaters were superb. *The Prince of Pilsen,* Rock and Fulton in *The Candy Shop,* Elizabeth Tyree in *Tit for Tat*, Lionel Barrymore as the boxer in Augustus Thomas' *The Other Girl* . . . gosh! I was taken to my first ball game, too, at the Polo Grounds (Mathewson pitching) and am one of the few men now alive who saw Ping Bodie try to steal home.

And the food! It is odd, considering how intensely spiritual I am, that that was about all I could talk about when I got back to London.

I took to American food from the start like a starving Eskimo flinging himself on a portion of blubber. The poet Keats, describing his emotions on first reading Chapman's Homer, speaks of himself as feeling like some watcher of the skies when a new planet swims into his ken. Precisely so did I feel that afternoon at Sherry's when the waiter brought me my first slab of strawberry shortcake. And the same goes for my subsequent introduction to shad roe, corned beef hash (with egg), buckwheat cakes and soft-shell crabs. "No matter if it puts an inch on my waistline," I said to myself, "I must be in on this."

I have been criticized for these exotic tastes of mine. English friends have told me that at the mere sight of a soft-shell crab their stomachs winced like salted snails and turned three handsprings. I don't argue with them. It is never any good arguing about other people's food. We may not be able to understand why a cannibal chief should like to tuck into the broiled missionary, but he does. The thing simply has to be accepted, just as we accept the fact that Scotsmen like haggis and Frenchmen *bouillabaisse*, though in *bouillabaisse* you are apt to find almost anything, from a nautical gentleman's sea boots to a china mug engraved with the legend "*Un cadeau*" (a present) *de* (from) *Deauville* (Deauville), while as for haggis . . .

How extraordinary it is, is it not, to reflect that each year as St. Andrew's Day comes around Scotsmen all over the world are sitting at dinner tables waiting with gleaming eyes for the arrival of this peculiar dish. Incredible as it may seem, they are looking forward to eating it. I applaud their rugged courage.

The fact that I regard haggis with dark suspicion is probably due to my having read Shakespeare. In my formative years I came across that bit in *Macbeth* and it established a complex. You remember the passage to which I refer? Macbeth comes upon the three witches while they are preparing the evening meal. They are dropping things into a caldron and chanting "Eye of newt and toe of frog, wool of bat and tongue of dog" and so on, and he immediately recognizes the recipe. "How now, you secret, black and midnight haggis," he cries, shuddering.

This has caused misunderstandings and has done an injustice to haggis. Grim as it is, it is not as bad as that—or should not be. What the dish really consists of—or should consist of—is the more intimate parts of a sheep, chopped up fine and blended with salt, pepper, nutmeg, onions, oatmeal and beef suet. But it seems to me that there is a grave danger of the cook going all whimsy and deciding not to stop there. When you reflect that the haggis is served up with a sort of winding sheet around it, concealing its contents, you will readily see that the temptation to play a practical joke on the boys must be almost irresistible. Scotsmen have their merry moods like all of us, and the thought must occasionally cross the cook's mind that it would be a great joke to shove in a lot of newts and frogs and bats and dogs and watch the gang wading into them.

Nor could the imposture be easily detected. The Athol brose which accompanies the haggis is a beverage composed of equal parts of whisky, cream and honey. After a glass or two of this you simply don't notice anything. I must confess that if I were invited to a St. Andrew's Day dinner, I would insist on taking the Public Analyst with me and turning my plate over to him before I touched a mouthful. My caution might cast a damper over the party. Censorious looks might be directed at me. I would not care. "Safety first," I would say to the Public Analyst. "Just analyze this, old man, will you?" And only when he had blown the All Clear would I consent to join the revels.

4

Back in London, I found that I had done wisely in going to New York even for so brief a visit. The manner of editors changed toward me. Where before it had been "Throw this man out," they now said, "Come in, my dear fellow, come in and tell us all about America." It is hard to believe in these days, when after breakfasting at the Berkeley you nip across the ocean and dine at the Stork Club, but in 1904 anybody in the writing world who had been to America was regarded with awe and looked on as an authority on that terra incognita. Well, when I tell you that a few weeks after my return the *Daily Chronicle* was paying me £1.5 for a review of *The Prince of Pilsen* and *Pearson's Weekly* two guineas for "Baseball" and "New York Crowds," I think I have made my point sufficiently clear.

I was branching out in other directions, too. In 1906 I got a job at the Aldwych Theater writing encore verses for the numbers in a musical comedy called *The Beauty of Bath*, and it was there one night that I was introduced to a small child—at least, he looked like a small child and was, I believe, eighteen—who was trying to break in as a composer and, so they told me, showed promise. His name was Jerome Kern. We wrote a topical song together for *The Beauty of Bath* called "Mister Chamberlain," and it was a riot. Six or seven encores every night. I don't know if Jerry made anything out of it. My end of the thing was included in my two pounds a week salary.

So, on the whole, I was doing quite nicely in my chosen walk of life. I made £505.1.7 in 1906 and £527.17.1 in 1907 and was living, I suppose, on about £203.4.9. In fact, if on November 17, 1907, I had not bought a Darracq car for £450 (and smashed it up in the first week) I should soon have been one of those economic royalists who get themselves so disliked. This unfortunate venture brought my capital back to about where it had started in 1904, and a long and dusty road had to be traveled before my finances were in a state sufficiently sound to justify another visit to America.

What took me there—in 1909—was Archie Fitzmaurice, and as I write that name the years fall away, hair sprouts on the vast bare steppes of my head, where never hair has been within the memory of the oldest inhabitant, and I am once more an eager young man going West in the hope—what a hope!—of getting nine hundred bucks out of Archibald Fitzmaurice, the painstaking and enthusiastic literary agent.

Archie Had Magnetism

Nicholas Boileau-Despréaux (1636–1711) once said, thereby getting himself into Bartlett's book of *Familiar Quotations,* "Every age has its pleasures, its style of wit, and its own ways." And, one might add, its own literary agents. It is one of the compensations of advancing years that time seems to bring with it bigger and better literary agents. When you arrive at the stage where the question of Japanese second serial rights crops up, you have generally got somebody looking after you who is incapable of pocketing a yen. But in one's early days, to get the cash from the outright sale of a short story to a magazine was a wonderful adventure. Especially if your affairs were in the capable hands of Archie Fitzmaurice.

My first dealings with Achie were through the medium of the post. It was a medium to which, as I shall show later, he did not always trust, but he did so on this occasion, and very charming letters he wrote. I had sent the MS. of a novel of mine, *Love among the Chickens,* to a friend on the New York *World*. Pressure of work compelled him to hand it over to a regular agent. He gave it to Archie. That was the expression he used in writing to me—"I have given it to Archie Fitzmaurice"—and I think Archie must have taken the word "given" literally. Certainly, when the book was published in America, it had on its title page, "Copyright by Archibald Fletcher Fitzmaurice" and a few years later, when the story was sold for motion pictures, I was obliged to pay him two hundred and fifty dollars to release it.

For the book was published in America. I will say that for Archie—he sold not only the book rights but also the serial rights and at a price which seemed to me fantastic. A thousand dollars it was, and to one who, like myself, had never got above fifty pounds for a serial and whose record royalties were £18.11.4, a thousand dollars was more than merely good. It was great gravy. It made the whole world seem different. A wave of gratitude to my benefactor swept over me. I felt like a man who has suddenly discovered a rich uncle from Australia.

There was just one flaw in my happiness. The money seemed a long time coming. In the letter (a delightful letter) in which he informed me of the sale, Archie said that a draft would arrive on October first. By Christmas I was inclined to restlessness. In March I cabled, and received a reply: "Letter explaining. Check immediately." Late in April the old restlessness returned, for no explaining letter had arrived. Toward the middle of May I decided to go to New York. In several of his letters Archie had told me I was the coming man. I came.

Archie entered my life heralded by a cloud of smoke and the penetrating aroma of one of the most spirited young cigars I have ever encountered; a little vulturelike man with green eyes, yellow hands, a blue suit, a red tie and gray hair. Quite a color scheme he presented that pleasant May morning.

"Say, listen," said Archie.

It was an interesting story that he had to tell. Where he had gone wrong, it seemed, was in trying to kill two birds with one stone. There was a charming girl of his acquaintance whom he had wanted me to meet, and he also wanted me to get my nine hundred dollars, and as this girl was leaving for England the happy idea struck him to give her the check to take to me. By doing this he would avoid all chance of having the letter get lost in the post and would enable his friend to meet me in circumstances where she would catch me at my best and sunniest—viz., while fingering a check for nine hundred dollars.

But what he had failed to take into account was that she would visit Monte Carlo on her way to England. . . .

There being no southern route in those days, this surprised me a little.

"Monte Carlo?" I said.

"Monte Carlo," said Archie.

"Monte *Carlo*?" I said.

"Monte Carlo," said Archie.

"But I didn't know . . ."

"Say, listen," said Archie.

He resumed his story. Yes, she had stopped over at Monte Carlo *en route*. But even then, mind you, it would have been all right if she had been by herself. She was a nice girl, who would never have dreamed of cashing a stranger's check. But her brother was with her, and he had fewer scruples. He gambled at the tables, and lost; borrowed his sister's jewelry, pawned it, and lost again. After that, there was nothing left for him to do but fall back on my check.

"But don't you worry," said Archie. "You shall be paid. I'll pay you myself. Yessir!"

And he gave me ten dollars and told me to get my hat and come along and see editors.

Archie had magnetism. There were moments before we separated when I almost believed that story and thought it very decent of him to let me have ten dollars. Ten dollars, I meant to say . . . just like that . . . right out of his own pocket. Pretty square.

His generalship was, I admit, consummate. He never ceased to keep moving. All that day we were dashing into elevators, dashing out, plunging into editorial offices, plunging out, leaping onto street cars, leaping out, till anything like rational and coherent thought was impossible.

He made only one tactical error. That was when he introduced me to the man to whom he had given my check.

He was an author from Kentucky. His experience had been practically identical with mine. He had sent his stories from Kentucky to a friend in New York, and the friend had handed them on to Archie, and Archie had sold them with magical skill, and then there had occurred that painful stage-wait in the matter of the cashing up. Eventually, when he was about twelve hundred dollars in the hole, the author, breathing hot Southern maledictions, packed a pistol and started for New York.

I think Archie must have been a little out of sorts the morning they met. The best he could do in the way of a story was to say he had lost the money on Wall Street. Later, he handed the Kentuckian the check he had received from the magazine for my novel, saying that he had sent me another for the same amount.

I did not see that there was anything to be done. New York at that time was full of men who did not see that there was anything to be done about Archie. He was so friendly about it all. When unmasked, he betrayed none of the baffled fury of the stage villain. He listened to you and considered the matter with his head on one side, like a vulture accused of taking an eyeball to which it was not entitled.

"Why, say, yes," he would observe at length. "Say, listen, I want to have a talk with you about that sometime."

You intimated that there was no time like the present. You pressed him. You were keen and resolute. And then somehow—for the life of you you could not say how—you found all of a sudden that the subject of your wrongs had been shelved and that you were accepting with every sign of good-fellowship a poisonous cigar from his vest pocket.

Yes, Archie had magnetism. Clients might come in upon him like lions, but they always went out like lambs. Not till they had been out from under his influence for a good hour or so did the realization of their imbecile weakness smite them, and then it was too late. His office, when they revisited it, was empty. He was off somewhere in the great open spaces, dashing into elevators, dashing out, plunging into editorial offices, plunging out, leaping into street cars, leaping out. And if by some miracle they did get hold of him, he just stuck his head on one side.

"Why, say, yes . . ."

And all the weary work started again.

I have often thought that King Henry the Eighth would have got on well with Archie. They had much in common. It was the practice of Henry the Eighth to "extort gifts from his subjects," which was exactly what Archie was so good at doing. The only difference between the two was that Henry appears to have confined his extorting to New Year's Day, whereas Archie was an all-the-year-round man.

I got my information about Henry the Eighth from the New Year article in the Encyclopaedia Britannica, and while doing so noticed, not for the first time, a very annoying habit of that great work of reference. I allude to the way it has of leaving off just at the point where it has got the reader all agog and excited. Thus, having mentioned that on New Year's Day, 1553, the bluff monarch got into the ribs of Cardinal Wolsey to the tune of one hundred and seventeen pounds, seventeen shillings and sixpence, it signs off, leaving the reader completely mystified. Why one-seventeen, seventeen and six? Why the seventeen bob? Why the sixpence?

The generally accepted explanation, that the King met the Cardinal in a dark alley on his way back from the bank and stood him on his head and lifted the contents of his pockets—£117.17.6—does not satisfy me. If Cardinal Wolsey had drawn a check to Self, it would have been for some less eccentric figure, and, knowing that it was New Year's Day and Henry was about, he would certainly not have gone to the bank without an armed escort. It is far more likely that he got separated from the money at the conclusion of a gay party in the small hours of the morning of January 1. The waiter came along with the death knell, and King Henry, after the usual unconvincing fumbling, told him to give it to the clerical gentleman over there in the paper hat, the one blowing the squeaker.

This would explain everything. The check came to a hundred and seventeen pounds, sixteen shillings. A shilling for the waiter and sixpence for the hat-check girl, and there you are.

Only one man ever got the better of Archie, and he, oddly enough, was not one of the tough story writers who were or had been reporters, fellows like Joe O'Brien or Charlie Somerville, but a poet. Those were the days when New York magazines had rather a weakness for short, crisp, uplift poems calling on the youth of America to throw its chest out and be up and doing with a heart for any fate. They would print these on their List of Contents page, accompanied by pictures of semi-nude men with hammers or hoes, or whatever it might be, and a magician like Archie could get a hundred dollars out of them per poem. He had got a hundred for one of this man's poems, which ran, if I remember correctly:

Be!
Be!
The past is dead,
Tomorrow is not born.
Be today!
Today!
Be with every nerve,
With every fiber,
With every drop of your red blood!
Be!
Be!

and he gave him his check for it, less the customary agent's ten per cent. The poet presented the check, and it bounced back at him.

You would have said that there was nothing to be done. Nor, in the case of a prose writer, would there have been. Undoubtedly I or Charles Neville Buck, my Kentucky friend, or any of the rest of Archie's stable would have treated the thing as a routine situation and handled it in the routine way, going around to see Archie—more as a matter of form than anything—and watching him put his head on one side and proceed through the "Why, say, yes" to the orthodox cigar.

But not the poet. Following his own advice, he decided that this was a moment to be with every nerve, with every fiber, with every drop of his red blood. He gave Archie's office boy fifty cents to nose about among Archie's papers and find out what his balance at the bank was. Having learned that it was $73.60, he paid in $16.40 to his account, presented the check again and cleaned him out. Archie never really got over that. He said it wasn't the money so much, it was the principle of the thing. It hurt him, the deceitfulness on the part of one on whom he had always looked almost as a son.

There are moments, when I am feeling particularly charitable, when I fancy that it was in that relationship that Archie regarded all of us bright young men. I tell myself that he meant well. He knew the temptations which New York holds for the young when they have money in their pockets, and he did all that in him lay to shield us from them. What he would really have liked would have been to hold a sort of patriarchal position to his clients. He owned a shack on Staten Island, and was always very urgent in inviting each new client to live there with him. His ideal, I believe, was to have the place full of eager youngsters, all working away at their stories and running to him when they wanted a little pocket money. He would have charge of all the cash accruing from their writings and would dole it out bit by bit as needed. He succeeded in inducing few young authors to see eye to eye with him in this matter.

Hi, Bartlett!

1

AT THE TIME of this second visit to New York I was still on the *Globe* doing the "By the Way" column, and had come over anticipating that after nineteen days I would have to tear myself away with many a longing lingering look behind and go back to the salt mines. But on the sixth day two strange things happened. I had brought with me a couple of short stories, and Archie sold one of them to *Cosmopolitan* for $200 and the other to *Collier's Weekly* for $300, both on the same morning. And—this is the second strange thing—he not only gave me the money, but waived his commission. Yes, that white—fairly white—man, though there were a dozen ways in which he could have used it himself, let me have the whole five hundred. Pretty heart-warming, I thought.

Another thought that came to me as I fingered the rustling bills and tried not to look at Archie, whose eyes were wet with unshed tears, for he had already started to regret, was that this was a good thing and wanted pushing along. I realized, of course, that New York was more expensive than London, but even so one could surely live there practically forever on five hundred dollars. Especially as there were always the good old *Cosmopolitan* and jolly old *Collier's Weekly* standing by with their cornucopias, all ready to start pouring. To seize pen and paper and mail my resignation to the *Globe* was with me the work of an instant. Then, bubbling over with hope and ambition, I took a room at the Hotel Duke down in Greenwich Village and settled in with a secondhand typewriter, paper, pencils, envelopes and Bartlett's book of *Familiar Quotations,* that indispensable adjunct to literary success.

I wonder if Bartlett has been as good a friend to other authors as he has been to me. I don't know where I would have been all these years without him. It so happens that I am not very bright and find it hard to think up anything really clever without assistance, but give me my Bartlett and I will slay you. How many an erudite little article of mine could not have been written without his never failing sympathy, encouragement and advice.

It has always been a puzzle to me how Bartlett did it, how he managed to compile a volume of three million quotations or whatever it is. One can see, of course, how he started. In its early stages the thing must have been reasonably simple. I picture him at a loose end one morning, going about shuffling his feet and whistling and generally messing around, and his mother said, "John, dear, I wish you wouldn't fidget like that. Why don't you find something to *do*?"

"Such as—?" said John Bartlett (born at Plymouth, Mass., in 1820).

"Dig in the garden."

"Don't want to dig in the garden."

"Or spin your top."

"Don't *want* to spin my top."

"Well, why not compile a book of familiar quotations, a collection of passages, phrases and proverbs, traced to their sources in ancient and modern literature?"

John Bartlett's face lit up. He lost that sullen look.

"Mater," he said, "I believe you've got something there. I'll do just that little thing. I see what you mean. 'To be or not to be,' and all that guff. Paper!" said John Bartlett. "Lots of paper, and can anyone lend me a pencil? California, here I come!"

So far, so good. But after that, what? Where did he go from there? You aren't going to tell me that he had all literature at his fingers' ends and knew just what Aldus Manutius said in 1472 and George M. Cohan in 1904. I suppose he went about asking people.

"Know anything good?" says John Bartlett, buttonholing an acquaintance.

"Shakespeare?"

"No, I've got Shakespeare."

"How about Pliny the Younger?"

"Never heard of him, but shoot."

"Pliny the Younger said, 'Objects which are usually the motives of our travels by land and by sea are often overlooked and neglected if they lie under our eye.' "

"He called that hot, did he?" says John Bartlett with an ugly sneer.

The acquaintance stiffens.

"If it was good enough for Pliny the Younger it ought to be good enough for a popeyed young pipsqueak born at Plymouth, Mass., in 1820."

"All right, all right, no need to get worked up about it. How are you on Pliny the Elder?"

"Pliny the Elder said, 'Everything is soothed by oil.' "

"Everything is what by *what*?"

"Soothed. By oil."

"Well, I'll bung it down," said John Bartlett dubiously, "but I don't think much of it. Ask me, the man must have been pie-eyed. Pliny the Elder should have kept off the sauce."

And so the book got written. In its original form it contained only 295 pages, but the latest edition which Christopher Morley has edited runs to one thousand two hundred and fifty-four, not counting 577 pages of index. It just shows how this quotation collecting grips you. You say to yourself that one more—as it might be "Guard us from error in narration" (Abu Mohammed Kasim Ben Ali Hariri, 1054–1122)—won't hurt you, and then you'll quit, but can you? Have you the will power to stop with Abu Mohammed Kasim Ben Ali Hariri and not go off on a regular toot with Bernard of Cluny (twelfth century) and Meir Ben Isaac Neherai (*circa* 1050)? Ah!

One rather unpleasant result of this continual bulging process is that Bartlett today has become frightfully mixed. It is like a conservative old club that has had to let down the barriers and let in a whole lot of rowdy young new members who lower the tone. There was a time when you couldn't get elected to Bartlett unless you were somebody like Richard Bethell, Lord Westbury (1800–1873), but now you never know who is going to pop out at you from its pages. Gabriel Romanovitch Derzhavin (1743–1816) often says to Alexis Charles Henri Clérel de Tocqueville (1805–1859) that it makes him good and sore.

"Heaven knows I'm no snob," he says, "but really when it comes to being expected to hobnob with ghastly outsiders like P. G. Wodehouse and the man who wrote 'Ain't It Awful, Mabel,' well, dash it!"

And Alexis Charles Henri says he knows exactly how Gabriel Romanovitch feels, and he has often felt the same way himself. They confess themselves at a loss to imagine what the world is coming to.

2

I was down having a nostalgic look at the Hotel Duke the other day, and was shocked to find that in the forty-six years during which I had taken my eye off it it had blossomed out into no end of a high-class joint with a Champagne Room or a Diamond Horseshoe or something like that where you can dance nightly to the strains of somebody's marimba band. In 1909 it was a seedy rookery inhabited by a group of young writers as impecunious as myself, and all the dancing we ever did resembled that of the lawyer in Gilbert and Sullivan who danced a dance in Westminster Court like a semidespondent fury, for he thought he never would hit on a chance of addressing a British jury. We did this when we found for the nth time that Archie Fitzmaurice was not going to part with that check of ours.

We paid weekly (meals included) about what you tip the waiter nowadays after a dinner for two, and it was lucky for me that the management did not charge more. If they had, I should have been in the red at the end of the first few months. For it was not long before I made the unpleasant discovery that my stuff, though bright and grammatical, was not everybody's dish. After that promising start both *Collier's* and the *Cosmopolitan* weakened and lost their grip. It was a year before I sold another one to *Collier's* and two before the *Cosmopolitan* got the right spirit again. If it had not been for the pulps—God bless them—I should soon have been looking like an Indian famine victim.

I have written elsewhere—in a book called *Heavy Weather*, if you don't mind me slipping in a quick plug—that the ideal toward which the City Fathers of all English country towns strive is to provide a public house for each individual inhabitant. It was much the same in the New York of 1909 as regarded the pulp magazines. There was practically one per person. They flooded the newsstands . . . *Munsey's*, the *Argosy*, the *All-Story*, the *Blue Book*, the *Green Book*, the *Topnotch*, *Adventure*, *Ainslee's*, the *Popular* and a hundred others. They all published the most ghastly slush, and they were nearly all edited by Robert H. Davis, a man who found no difficulty in springing from pulp to pulp like the chamois of the Alps from crag to crag.

I have heard Bob Davis described as a hard-boiled editor, but he never struck me in that light. More like an angel in human shape he seemed to me. It was entirely owing to him that I was able to eat at all in the years when I first became a resident of New York.

Plots were my trouble. I was handicapped as a writer by the fact that I knew nothing about anything. All the other members of my circle had backgrounds on which they could draw. Charles Neville Buck had fraternized with Kentucky mountaineers since childhood, and could produce feud stories like rabbits out of a hat. Charlie Somerville was a reporter. Roy Norton had been with Rex Beach in the Klondike. I alone had nothing to write about except what I could dig out of a brain which has never amounted to much at the best of times. The typewriter clattering in the room on the right showed that Charles Neville Buck had got to the part where Big Hank Hawkins is saying to an acquaintance whom he had never much liked: "Gol durn yuh, Rupe Tolliver, for a sneakin', ornery, low-down, double-crossin', hornswogglin' skunk. Git out of these hyah hills or I'll drill yuh like a dog." The one clattering in the room on the left indicated that Roy Norton was back again in the dance halls of Dawson City. And where was Wodehouse? Just sitting there twiddling his fingers. I had a certain facility for dialogue and a nice light comedy touch—at least, I thought it was nice—but what I needed was plots, and just as I was thinking I would never get another one, I met Bob Davis.

Bob was terrific. I would look in at his office on top of the Flatiron Building and find him at an enormous desk littered with papers, a smallish, almost circular man who seemed to be quivering like a dynamo all the time with suppressed nervous force, of which he must have had plenty. Anyone who is editing fifty-seven or whatever it was simultaneous pulps has need of nervous force, especially if he has that legendary figure "Mr. Munsey" getting in his hair from nine in the morning till six in the evening. After a few civil exchanges—I saying "Good morning, Mr. Davis" and he damning my eyes for interrupting his work—he would get down to business.

"What on earth have you been doing all these weeks? I haven't seen a line of yours. Why aren't you writing?"

"I can't get a plot."

"Can't get a plot? Can't get a *plot*? How do you mean, you can't get a plot?"

"There aren't any."

"What sort of plot do you want?"

"Any sort of plot."

"Wait!"

He springs from behind the desk and starts to pace the room. Two turns up and down and words begin to flutter from him like bats out of a barn. Five minutes later I have the plot complete. It is probably a frightful plot and I am going to blush all the time I am writing it up, but for the completed story I shall get at least fifty and possibly seventy-five dollars.

For I was lucky to meet Bob at a time when Mr. Munsey's ideas of payment had become more lavish than they had been in the nineties. Albert Payson Terhune in his *To the Best of My Memory* tells of selling a sixty-thousand-word serial to Bob and getting $125 for it. The only full-length novel I wrote for him brought me what *Variety* would call a hotsy $2,000 and enabled me to live like a prince for a year.

Bob needed handling. He tended at times to be fussy and

a perfectionist. You had to take your stuff back quite often and fix it. But much could be done with tact. Terhune discovered this. He says:

> I had sent him a yarn, and he had asked me to come to his office and talk it over with him. He told me there was something radically wrong with the upbuilding of the story; something he could not put his finger on but which was sharply apparent to him. He bade me take it home and pore over it and then rewrite it from a new angle.
>
> I took it home and I left it unread and untouched, in its envelope, for ten days. Then, without changing so much as a comma, I sent it back to him. Promptly came an acceptance, together with a note from Davis saying that I had done clever work in smoothing out the story's kinks and readjusting its angle, and that now it was wholly satisfactory. His letter ended by saying this was a proof of the advantage of taking one's time and of rewriting a tale after putting it aside for a while.

3

I wrote every kind of story for Bob. I even wrote a series of whodunits, and got a nasty shock a month or two ago when one of them appeared in one of those reprint magazines, for I had hoped that my shame was buried in the mists of time.

Not that I have anything against whodunits. Very few of them are as bad as mine. But Bob always insisted on a love interest, and where he got the idea that anyone wants a girl messing about and getting in the way when the automatics are popping I could never understand. Nobody has a greater respect than myself for girls in their proper place—if I went to a night club and found no girls there, I should be the first to complain—but I maintain that they have no business in Lascar Joe's Underground Den in Limehouse on a busy evening. Apart from anything else, Woman seems to me to lose her queenly dignity when she is being shoved into closets with a bag over her head. And something of that sort is always happening to the heroine of a goose-flesher.

For, though beautiful, with large gray eyes and hair the color of ripe wheat, she is never a very intelligent girl. She may have escaped death a dozen times. She knows the Blackbird Gang is after her to get the papers. The police may have warned her on no account to stir outside her house. But when a messenger calls at half-past two in the morning with an unsigned note saying "Come at once," she just reaches for her hat and goes. The messenger is a one-eyed half-breed with a pock-marked face and an evil grin, so she trusts him immediately and, having accompanied him into the closed car with steel shutters over the windows, bowls off in it to the ruined cottage in the swamp. And when the hero, at great risk and inconvenience to himself, comes to rescue her, she will have nothing to do with him because she has been told by a mulatto with half a nose that it was he who murdered her brother Jim.

This girl must go. What we all liked about Sherlock Holmes was his correct attitude in this matter of girls in mystery stories. True, he would permit them to call at Baker Street and tell him about the odd behavior of their uncles and stepfathers—at a pinch he might even allow them to marry Watson—but once the story was under way they had to retire into the background and stay there.

The obvious person, of course, to rid us of these girls is the villain, but experience has taught us that we cannot rely on this man. He has let us down too often, and forfeited our confidence.

The trouble with the villain of what is now called the story of suspense is that he suffers from a fatal excess of ingenuity. When he was a boy, his parents must thoughtlessly have told him that he was clever, and it has absolutely spoiled him for effective work.

The ordinary man, when circumstances compel him to murder a female acquaintance, borrows a pistol and does the thing in some odd five minutes of the day when he is not at the office or the pictures. He does not bother about art or technique or scientific methods. He just goes and does it. But the villain cannot understand simplicity. It never occurs to him just to point a gun at the heroine and fire it. If you told him the thing could be done that way, he would suspect you of kidding him. The only method he can imagine is to tie her in a chair, erect a tripod, place the gun on it, tie a string to the trigger, pass the string along the walls till it rests on a hook, attach another string to it, pass this over a hook, tie a brick to the second string and light a candle under it. He has got the thing reasoned out. The candle will burn the second string, the brick will fall, and the weight will tighten the first string, thus pulling the trigger and completing a neat job.

Then somebody comes along and blows the candle out. I have known a villain to sit the heroine on a keg of gunpowder and expect it to be struck by lightning. You can't run a business that way.

Still, I suppose it is no use getting cross with the poor fellows. They are doing their best according to their lights. It is simply that they are trying to tackle a highly specialized job without the requisite training. What the villain needs to do is to forget all he thinks he knows and go right back to the beginning and start learning his ABC. He requires careful schooling.

The keynote of the curriculum of this school for villains would be the inculcation of simplicity and directness. For quite a while he would confine himself to swatting flies. The average villain's impulse, if called upon to kill a fly, would be to saw away the supports of the floor, tie a string across the doorway, and then send the fly an anonymous letter telling it to come at once in order to hear of something to its advantage. The idea being that it would hurry to the room, trip over the string, fall on the floor, tumble into the depths and break its neck.

That, to the villain's mind, is not merely the simplest, it is the only way of killing flies. And the hardest task facing the kindergarten authorities would be to persuade him that excellent results may be obtained through the medium of a rolled-up copy of the *Saturday Evening Post*. What these men have got to learn is that the best way of disposing of a girl with hair the color of ripe wheat is to hit that hair as hard as possible with a section of gas pipe. Buying scorpions to put in her bag or little-known Asiatic poisons with which to smear her lipstick does no good whatever and only adds to the overhead.

Put Me among the Earls

1

WELL, what with this and what with that, all right so far, I felt, but the fact that I was able to pay my weekly bill at the Duke and could sometimes—very occasionally—lunch at the Brevoort did not satisfy me. I wanted something much more in the nature of a Horatio Alger success story, and I would be deceiving my public if I were to say that I did not chafe. I chafed very frequently. "What are you making of this life of yours, Wodehouse?" I would often say to myself, and it seemed to me that the time had come to analyze and evaluate my position with a view to taking prompt steps through the proper channels.

Quite suddenly I spotted what was wrong. It came to me like a flash one morning when I was having a malted milk shake at the drugstore around the corner. I had been labeling my stories "by P. G. Wodehouse" and this at a time when a writer who went about without three names was practically going around naked. Those were the days of Richard Harding Davis, of Margaret Culkin Banning, of James Warner Bellah, of Earl Derr Biggers, of Charles Francis Coe, Norman Reilly Raine, Mary Roberts Rinehart, Clarence Budington Kelland and Orison Swett—yes, really, I'm not kidding—Marden. And here was I, poor misguided fool, trying to crash the gate with a couple of contemptible initials.

No wonder the slicks would not take my work. In anything like a decent magazine I would have stood out as conspicuously as a man in a seersucker suit at the first night of the Opera.

It frequently happens that when you get an inspiration, you don't stop there but go right ahead and get another. It was so with me now. Scarcely had the last remains of the milk shake gurgled up through the straw when I was telling myself that I had been all wrong in thinking that I knew nothing about anything. I knew quite a lot about English country-house life with its earls and butlers and younger sons, and it was quite possible—though I recognized this question as a very moot one—that the American magazine public would like to read about them. Worth trying, anyway.

Two days later I was typing on a clean white page

SOMETHING NEW
BY
PELHAM GRENVILLE WODEHOUSE

And I had a feeling that I was going to hit the jackpot. It seemed incredible to me that all this while I should have been chucking away an income-producing combination like Pelham Grenville Wodehouse. It put me right up there with Harry Leon Wilson, David Graham Phillips, Arthur Somers Roche and Hugh McNair Kahler.

If you ask me to tell you frankly if I like the name Pelham Grenville Wodehouse, I must confess that I do not. I have my dark moods when it seems to me about as low as you can get. I was named after a godfather, and not a thing to show for it but a small silver mug. But I was born at a time when children came to the font not knowing what might not happen to them before they were dried off and taken home. My three brothers were christened respectively Philip Peveril, Ernest Armine and Lancelot Deane, so I was probably lucky not to get something wished on me like Hyacinth Augustus or Albert Prince Consort. And say what you will of Pelham Grenville, shudder though you may at it, it changed the luck. *Something New* was bought as a serial by the *Saturday Evening Post*, and they paid me three thousand five hundred dollars for it, if you can believe there is that much money in the world. It was the first of the series which I may call the Blandings Castle Saga, featuring Clarence, ninth Earl of Emsworth, his son the Hon. Freddie Threepwood and his butler Beach, concerning whom I have since written so much.

Too much, carpers have said. So have cavilers, and they are probably correct. Except for the tendency to write articles about the Modern Girl and allow his side-whiskers to grow, there is nothing an author today has to guard himself against more carefully than the Saga habit. He writes a story. Another story dealing with the same characters occurs to him, and he writes that. He feels that just one more won't hurt him, and he writes a third. And before he knows it, he is down with a Saga and no cure in sight.

This is what happened to me with Lord Emsworth and the Blandings Castle set and later on with Jeeves and Bertie Wooster. Beginning with *Something New*, I went on to *Leave It to Psmith*, then to *Fish Preferred*, after that to *Heavy Weather*, *Blandings Castle*, *The Crime Wave at Blandings*, *Uncle Fred in the Springtime*, *Full Moon* and *Pigs Have Wings*. And to show the habit-forming nature of the drug, while it was eight years after *Something New* before the *Leave It to Psmith* urge gripped me, only eighteen months elapsed between *Fish Preferred and Heavy Weather*.

In a word, once a man who could take it or leave it alone, I had become an addict.

2

A critic, with whose name I will not sully my typewriter—he has probably by now been eaten by bears like the children who made mock of the prophet Elisha—was giving me the sleeve across the windpipe the other day for this tendency of mine to write so much about members of the British peerage. Specifically, he accused me of an undue fondness for earls.

Well, of course, now that I come to tot up the score, I realize that in the course of my literary career I have featured quite a number of these fauna, but as I often say—well, perhaps once a month—why not? I see no objection to earls. A most respectable class of men they seem to me. And one admires their spirit. I mean, while some, of course, have come up the easy way, many have had the dickens of a struggle starting at the bottom of the ladder as mere Hons., having to go in to dinner after the Vice-Chancellor of the Duchy of Lancaster and all that sort of thing.

Show me the Hon. who by pluck and determination has raised himself from the depths, step by step, till he has become entitled to keep a coronet on the hat peg in the downstairs closet, and I will show you a man of whom any author might be proud to write.

Put Me among the Earls

Earls on the whole have made a very good showing in fiction. With baronets setting them a bad example by being almost uniformly steeped in crime, they have preserved a gratifying high standard of behavior. There is seldom anything wrong with the earl in fiction, if you don't mind a touch of haughtiness and a tendency to have heavy eyebrows and draw them together in a formidable frown, like the one in *Little Lord Fauntleroy*. And in real life I can think of almost no earls whose hearts were not as pure and fair as those of dwellers in the lowlier air of Seven Dials.

Oh yes. Earl Carroll. He caused a lot of talk in New York some years ago by giving a party at which a girl took a bath in champagne with, if I have the story rightly, not so much as a Bikini bathing suit on. But he was not a member of the peerage, he was a theatrical producer.

English literature, lacking earls, would have been a great deal poorer. Shakespeare would have been lost without them. Everyone who has writen for the theater knows how difficult it is to get people off the stage unless you can think of a good exit speech. That is why, as you pass through Greenwich Village and other literary quarters, you see haggard men wandering about and sticking straws in their hair as they mutter:

"Life, dear lady, is like . . ."
"Life, dear lady . . ."
"Dear lady, I have but two objections to life . . . One is that it . . ."

Than which nothing is sadder.

Shakespeare had no such problem. With more earls than he knew what to do with, he was on velvet. One need only quote those well-known lines from his Henry VII, Part One:

> My Lord of Sydenham, bear our royal word
> To Brixton's Earl, the Earl of Wormwood Scrubs,
> Our faithful liege, the Earl of Dulwich (East),
> And those of Beckenham, Penge and Peckham Rye,
> Together with the Earl of Hampton Wick;
> Bid them to haste like cats when struck with brick,
> For they are needed in our battle line,
> And stitch in time doth ever save full nine.
> *(Exeunt Omnes. Trumpets and hautboys.)*

"Pie!" Shakespeare used to say to Burbage, and Burbage would agree that Shakespeare earned his money easily.

A thing about earls I have never understood, and never liked to ask anyone for fear of betraying my ignorance, is why one earl is the Earl of Whoosis and another earl just Earl Smith. I have an idea—I may be wrong—that the "of" boys have a social edge on the others, like the aristocrats in Germany who are able to call themselves "Von." One can picture the Earl of Berkeley Square being introduced to Earl Piccadilly at a cocktail party. The host says, "Oh, Percy, I want you to meet Earl Piccadilly," and hurries away to attend to his other guests. There is a brief interval during which the two agree that this is the rottenest party they were ever at and possibly exchange a remark or two about the weather, then the Earl of Berkeley Square says, "I didn't quite get the name. Earl of Piccadilly, did he say?"

"No, just Earl Piccadilly."

The Earl of Berkeley Square starts. A coldness creeps into his manner.

"You mean *plain* Earl Piccadilly?"

"That's right."

"No 'of'?"

"No, no 'of.' "

There is a tense silence. You can see the Earl of Berkeley Square's lip curling.

"Ah, well," he says at length, with a nasty little snigger, "it takes all sorts to make a world, does it not?" and Earl Piccadilly slinks off with his ears pinned back and drinks far too many martinis in the hope of restoring his self-respect. Practically all the earls who are thrown sobbing out of cocktail parties are non-*of*s. They can't take it, poor devils.

3

Twenty-one of my books were serialized in the *Saturday Evening Post*. For the first one, as I say, I received $3,500, for the second they raised me to $5,000, for the third to $7,500, for the fourth to $10,000. That was when I felt safe in going back to "P. G. Wodehouse."

It caused, of course, a good deal of consternation in the office. I am not sure whether there was a sharp drop in the circulation and advertisement figures, but the boys in Independence Square were badly shaken. Nevertheless, for the last twelve I got $40,000 per. Nice going, of course, and the stuff certainly came in handy, but I have always been alive to the fact that I am not one of the real big shots. I don't expect to go down in legend and song. I don't get nearly enough letters from admirers.

As everybody knows, an author's standing is estimated by the number of letters he receives from readers. It is the equivalent of the Hooper rating of television, and I have often felt sorry for men like Cicero and Diogenes Laertius, who wrote in the days before the post office came into existence. They could never tell for certain when they had pushed their work across and made a solid hit with the public.

Diogenes Laertius, of course, had a few friends who thought he was great—or, at any rate, told him so when they had made quite sure he was picking up the tab for the round of Falernian wine, and sometimes a kindly senator would pat Cicero on the shoulder in the Campus Martius and say "I liked that last little thing of yours, Tullius, I can't remember what it was called. Are you writing anything now?" But getting right down to it, they were simply working in the dark, and it must have been discouraging for them.

There is no point on which your modern author is more

touchy than this thing of testimonials from the public. You will see John P. Marquand saunter up to Erle Stanley Gardner and speak with an ill-assumed carelessness.

"You don't happen to know of a good secretary, do you, Stan?" he says. "I've been caught short, confound it. Mine has just got typist's cramp, answering letters from admirers of my books, and more pouring in daily."

"John," says Erle Stanley Gardner, "you know me. If I could help you out, I would do it like a shot. But I'm in just the same jam myself. Both my secretaries collapsed this morning and are in hospital with ice packs on their heads. I've never known the fan mail heavier."

"Look here," say Marquand abruptly, "how many fan letters did you get last week?"

"How many did you?" says Gardner.

"I asked you first," says Marquand, and they part on bad terms.

And in another corner of the room Mickey Spillane rising and walking away in a marked manner from Frances Parkinson Keyes.

Going by this test, I should describe myself as a sort of fair to medium, not on the one hand a socko and yet, on the other, not laying a definite egg. The books I write seem to appeal to a rather specialized public. Invalids read me. So do convicts. And I am all right with the dog stealers. As regards Obuasie I am not so sure.

From Obuasie (wherever that is) there reached me a short while ago the following letter:

DEAR SIR.

I have heard your name and address highly have been recommended to me by a certain friend of mine that you are the best merchant in your city New York. So I want you to send me one of your best catalogues and I am ready to deal with you until I shall go into the grave. Soon as possible send me early.

Now it is difficult to know just what to make of a letter like that. At first glance it would seem as if I had Obuasie in my pocket. But there is always the possibility that some confusion has arisen and that my correspondent is under the impression that I deal in something quite different from what I do deal in, whatever you may call it. Misunderstandings so easily occur at a distance. One remembers the story of the drummer who traveled in cement docks and would often dash halfway across the world on hearing that there was a demand for his wares in Tierra del Fuego or Spitzbergen, only to discover, after he had dragged his bag of samples all that weary way, that what the natives wanted was not docks but socks.

Better, perhaps, then, for the moment not to get my publishers to flood Obuasie with my books, but to stick to the invalids and the convicts, who, with the dog stealers, surely make up a public quite large enough for any author who is not utterly obsessed by the lust for gold. Money isn't everything.

My popularity with invalids puts me in something of a quandary. Naturally I like my stories to be read as widely as possible, but, kindhearted by nature, I do not feel altogether happy when I gather that some form of wasting sickness is an essential preliminary to their perusal. And such seems to be the case.

I can understand it, of course. When you are fit and strong, you go about with your chin up and your chest out, without a single morbid tendency. "I feel great," you say, "so why should I deliberately take the sunshine out of life by reading Wodehouse?" And you don't. But comes a day when the temperature begins to mount, the tonsils to ache and dark spots to float before the eyes. Then somehow or other you find one of my books by your bedside, and the next thing you know you are reading it. And you go on reading it till health and sanity return.

It is not difficult to see what a dilemma this places me in. I need readers, and in order to have readers I must have invalids. And as soon as they become convalescent, I lose them. If you want to see a mind in a ferment of doubt and indecision, take a look at mine when the papers announce that another epidemic has broken out and hundreds are taking to their beds. One moment I am thinking how sad it all is, the next saying "My Public!" and wondering what the royalties will amount to.

But, you will say, why bother about the invalids if you have the dog stealers behind you? And here I am faced by a somewhat embarrassing confession. When I said I was read by dog stealers, I was swanking. It is not a solid *bloc* of dog stealers who enjoy my work, but one solitary dog stealer and—a galling thought—a rotten dog stealer at that, for he specifically admits to having been arrested and imprisoned. And, further, I cannot help feeling that his motives in writing to me were mixed. It was not, I suspect, simply a gush of admiration for my artistry that led him to pen that letter but also the hope—expressed in his letter—that I would give him a sum of money sufficient to enable him to start a street bookmaker's business. And even if I am wronging him in this the outlook seems to me most unpromising. The more I think over his letter, the less confident do I feel that the man is going to be a steady source of income to me down the years.

It is no good kidding oneself. The way I figure it out is that in order to buy my books he will have to steal dogs, and he will certainly not steal dogs in anything like the necessary quantity unless he develops considerably more skill and know-how than he now possesses. He might have a good year, when the dogs came briskly in and he felt himself in a position not only to buy his own copy but to send others as birthday presents to his friends, but the chances are far greater that his crude and bungling methods will lead to another arrest, and what use will he be to me, shut off from the bookstores just when my new novel needs support to make it go? As a commercial proposition I can only write him down as shaky, and it would probably be sounder bookkeeping to take him out of the dog-stealer column and lump him in with the convicts.

I have had so many letters over the years from convicts that I have begun to think that the American criminal must look on one or more of my works as an essential part of his kit. I seem to see the burglar's mother sending him off for the night shift.

"Another glass of hot milk, Clarence?"

"No, thank you, Mother. I must be going."

"Yes, it is getting late. Are you well wrapped up?"

"Yes, Mother."

"Wearing your warm underclothing?"

"Yes, Mother."

"Have you everything you need? Gat? Brass knucks? Wodehouse novel? Oxyacetylene blowpipe? Trinitrotoluol? Mask?"

"Yes, Mother."

"Then heaven speed you, boy, and always remember what your dear father used to say: 'Tread lightly, read your Wodehouse, save your pennies and the dollars will take care of themselves.' "

There was a bank robber in Chicago not long ago who in a fit of preoccupation caused by business worries imprudently took with him by mistake a book of light essays by Frank Sullivan. The shock of discovering his blunder, when he opened the volume to go on with Chapter Eleven, so unnerved him that he missed the policeman at three yards and was expelled from his gang in disgrace. You cannot be too careful if you wish to succeed in a difficult and overcrowded profession.

The Meteorite Racket

1

BUT THOUGH my public is, as I have said, a limited one, I have never been sorry that I became a writer. Taking it by and large, I have not done so badly. Certainly a good deal better than I would have done in some of the other professions. I am thinking at the moment of the secondhand bridge business, snail-gathering and getting hit in the stomach by meteorites.

The secondhand bridge racket attracts many because at first sight it looks like finding money in the street. You get anything from $125,000 for a used bridge, but—and here is the catch—it is by no means everybody who wants a used bridge. They were trying to sell the one on Third Avenue over the Harlem River the other day, and despite all the efforts of the auctioneers to sales-talk the customers into scaring the moths out of their pocketbooks no one would bid a nickel for it.

It was a good bridge, too. It had four trusses and between the trusses three lanes for vehicular traffic, and was capable of carrying a hundred thousand vehicles and five hundred thousand pedestrians daily. "Give it to your girl for Christmas and watch her face light up," said the advertisements, but nothing doing. It went begging.

Snail-gathering, which flourishes mostly in Austria, if you can call it flourishing, is another profession into which I doubt if I would put any son of mine. I was shocked to learn the other day that the Austrian boys who track the creatures down get only a shilling a pound for them. (It should be schilling, but I can't do the dialect.)

I don't know how many snails go to the pound, for it must vary a good deal according to their size and robustness. You get great, big, hulking snails, the sort of snails whose friends call them Butch and Fatso, and conversely you get wan, wizened little snails which have stunted their growth with early cigarette-smoking. But, be that as it may, two or three hundred pounds of them must take quite a bit of assembling, and I think that what the Austrians call schnirkel-schnecke gatherers come under the head of sweated labor. Yet Austrian fathers are rather pleased when their sons tell them that that is the walk in life which they have chosen.

"Pop," say the Austrian son, "I want to be a schnirkel-schnecke gatherer."

"Capital, capital (*Das Kapital, Das Kapital*)," says the Austrian father, and tells him to start right in.

A misguided policy, it seems to me, because when the schnirkel-schneckes are sold to a French restaurant, the French restaurant gets about $280.01 for the same amount of schnirkel-schneckes for which the schnirkel-schnecke gatherer got about $27.45, leaving the latter down a matter of $252.56. (Check these figures.) Obviously what the boy ought to do is get a job in a French restaurant, marry the boss's daughter and become part proprietor.

I don't see there is much future, either, in the getting-hit-in-the-stomach-by-meteorites racket.

Yes, I know what you are going to say. You are going to tell me that down in Sylacauga, Alabama, last year, Mrs. Ann Elizabeth Hodges, as she lay on the sofa in her living room, was hit in the stomach by a meteorite which came in via the roof, and sold it—the meteorite—for $2,700 to a Montana museum.

"Reason it out," I can hear you saying. "Two thousand seven hundred smackers, and all that from one meteorite, mark you. A meteorite a day—"

"—keeps the doctor away. True. So far I am with you. But——"

"At $2,700 per meteorite per person per day, that would

be $985,500 a year—or in Leap Year $988,200. That's nice money."

"Ah," I reply, "but have you considered that whole days might pass without your getting hit in the stomach by a meteorite? They are most unreliable things. Capricious. You can't count on them. There must be dozens of people in America who have not been hit in the stomach by a meteorite and quite likely will not be."

"I never thought of that," you say, and you go off and become an average adjuster and do well.

And meanwhile Mrs. Ann Elizabeth Hodges, in the suit of chain mail which she now habitually wears, is lying on her sofa in Sylacauga, Alabama, looking up at the ceiling and hoping for the best. Good luck, Mrs. Hodges. I think you are living in a fool's paradise, but nevertheless good luck.

2

Yes, I am glad I stuck to writing, even though I have never succeeded in reaching the heights. I suppose, if you come right down to it, that I am to Literature about what Pinky Lee is to Television. I go in for what is known in the trade as "light writing," and those who do that—humorists they are sometimes called—are looked down upon by the intelligentsia and sneered at. One of them of my acquaintance was referred to in a weekly paper not long ago as "that burbling pixie." Well, you can't go calling a man a burbling pixie without lowering his morale. He frets. He refuses to eat his cereal. He goes about with his hands in his pockets, kicking stones. The next thing you know, he is writing thoughtful novels analyzing social conditions, and you are short another humorist. With things going the way they are, it won't be long before the species dies out. Already what was once a full-throated chorus has faded into a few scattered chirps. Now and then you can still hear from the thicket the gay note of the Perelman, piping as the linnets do, but Perelman can't go on forever, and then what?

I recently edited an anthology of the writings of American humorists, and was glad to do so, for I felt that such publications ought to be encouraged. Publish an anthology of their writings, and you revive the poor drooping souls like watered flowers. The pleasant surprise of finding that somebody loves them makes them feel that it is not such a bad little world after all, and they pour their dose of strychnine back into the bottle and go out into the sunlit street through the door instead of, as they had planned, through the seventh-story window. Being asked for contributions to the book I have mentioned was probably the only nice thing that had happened to these lepers since 1937.

Three suggestions as to why "light writing" has almost ceased to be have been made—one by myself, one by the late Russell Maloney and one by Wolcott Gibbs. Here is mine for what it is worth.

Humorists, as I see it, have always been looked askance at, if not actually viewed with concern. At English schools in my boyhood they were divided into two classes, both unpopular. If you merely talked amusingly, you were a "silly ass." ("You *are* a silly ass!" was the formula.) If your conversation took a mordant and satirical turn, you were a "funny swine." And whichever you were, you were scorned and despised and lucky not to get kicked. It is to this early discouragement that I attribute the fact that no Englishman, grown to man's estate, ever says anything brighter than "Eh, what?" and "Most extraordinary."

Russell Maloney's theory is that a humorist has to be a sort of dwarf. In the Middle Ages, he points out, the well-bred and well-to-do considered nothing so funny as a man who was considerably shorter than they were, or at least cultivated a deceptive stoop. Today the humors of maladjustment have succeeded the humors of deformity, and they want you to be neurotic. If you aren't neurotic, you simply don't rate. And the reason why there are so few humorists nowadays is that it is virtually impossible to be neurotic when you have only to smoke any one of a dozen brands of cigarettes or eat any one of a dozen brands of breakfast food to be in glowing health both physically and mentally. If I have tried once to be neurotic, I have tried a hundred times, but no luck. Just when I thought I was beginning to get somewhere, I would smoke a Fortunate or take a spoonful of Cute Crispies, and back to where I had started.

What Wolcott Gibbs thinks—and what Wolcott Gibbs thinks today Manchester thinks tomorrow—is that the

shortage is due to the fact that the modern tendency is to greet the humorist, when he dares to let out a bleat, with a double whammy from a baseball bat. In the past ten years, he says, the humorist has become increasingly harried and defensive, increasingly certain that the minute he raises his foolish head the hot-eyed crew will be after him, denouncing him as a fiddler while Rome burns. Naturally after one or two experiences of this kind he learns sense.

Gibbs, I think, is right. Humorists have been scared out of the business by the touchiness now prevailing in every section of the community.

"Never," said Robert C. Ruark in the *World-Telegram* not long ago, "have I heard so much complaining as I have heard this year. My last month's mail has contained outraged yelps on pieces I have written concerning dogs, diets, ulcers, cats and kings. I wrote a piece laughing at the modern tendency of singers to cry, and you would have thought I had assaulted womanhood."

A few days before the heavyweight championship fight between Rocky Marciano and Roland La Starza, an Australian journalist who interviewed the latter was greatly struck by his lucid replies to questions.

"Roland," he wrote, "is a very intelligent young man. He has brains. Though it may be," he added, "that I merely think he has because I have been talking so much of late to tennis players. Tennis players are just one cut mentally above the wallaby."

I have never met a wallaby, so cannot say from personal knowledge how abundantly—or poorly—equipped such animals are with the little gray cells, but of one thing I am sure and that is that letters poured in on the writer from Friends of the Wallaby, the International League for Promoting Fair Play for Wallabies and so on, protesting against the injustice of classing them lower in the intellectual scale than tennis players. Pointing out, no doubt, that while the average run-of-the-mill wallaby was perhaps not an Einstein, it would never dream of bounding about the place shouting "Forty love" and similar ill-balanced observations.

I don't know what is to be done about it. It is what the French would call an impasse. Only they say amh-parrse. Silly, of course, but you know what Frenchmen are. (And now to await the flood of stinkers from Faure, Pinay, Maurice Chevalier, Mendès-France, Oo-La-La and Indignant Parisienne.)

They say it is possible even today to be funny about porcupines and remain unscathed, but I doubt it. Just try it and see how quickly you get a stream of letters beginning:

> "SIR:
>
> With reference to your recent tasteless and uncalled-for comments on the porcupine . . ."

A writer in one of the daily papers was satirical the other day about oysters, and did he get jumped on! A column-long letter next morning from Oyster Lover, full of the bitterest invective. And the same thing probably happened to the man who jocularly rebuked a trainer of performing fleas for his rashness in putting them through their paces while wearing a beard. Don't tell me there is not some league or society for the protection of bearded flea trainers watching over their interests and defending them from ridicule.

In short, I do not think I am putting it too strongly when I say that things have come to a pretty pass.

"What we need in this country," said Robert Benchley in one of his thoughtful essays, "is fewer bridges and more fun." And how right he was, as always. We have the Triborough Bridge, the George Washington Bridge, the Fifty-ninth Street Bridge, auction bridge, contract bridge, Senator Bridges and Bridgehampton, Long Island, but where's the fun?

When I first came to America, everyone was gay and

lighthearted. Each morning and evening paper had its team of humorists turning out daily masterpieces in prose and verse. Magazines printed a couple of funny short stories and a comic article in every number. Publishers published humorous books. It was the golden age, and I think it ought to be brought back. I want to see an S. J. Perelman on every street corner, a Bob Benchley in every drugstore. It needs only a little resolution on the part of the young writers and a touch of the old broad-mindedness among editors.

And if any young writer with a gift for being funny has got the idea that there is something undignified and antisocial about making people laugh, let him read this from the Talmud, a book which, one may remind him, was written in an age just as grim as this one.

> . . . And Elijah said to Berokah "These two will also share in the world to come." Berokah then asked them "What is your occupation?" They replied "We are merrymakers. When we see a person who is downcast, we cheer him up." These two were among the very select few who would inherit the Kingdom of Heaven.

To the Critics, These Pearls

1

I HAD scarcely typed that passage referring to the critic who complained of my writing too much about earls when I opened a weekly paper and darned if another critic hadn't started a second front and was complaining of my writing too much about butlers. "It is time that Mr. Wodehouse realized," he said, "that Jeeves has become a bore." (Not that Jeeves is a butler. He is a gentleman's personal gentleman.) I shall, of course, reply to this hellhound the moment I can get around to it, and I shall not mince my words.

Having now reached the stage—one foot in the grave

and the other not far off it—where I can legitimately get pompous and start giving advice to the youngsters, I would urge what are sometimes called commencing authors to make up their minds as soon as possible as to what is to be their attitude toward the critics.

Many people would counsel the young author to ignore hostile criticism, but to my thinking this is cowardly and he will be missing a lot of fun. An unfavorable review should be answered promptly with a carefully composed letter, which can be either (a) conciliatory or (b) belligerent.

Specimen A. The Conciliatory

Dear Mr. Worthington,

Not "Sir." "Sir" is abrupt. And, of course, don't say "Mr. Worthington" if the fellow's name is Schwartz or Heffelfinger. Use your intelligence, Junior. I am only sketching the thing out on broad lines.

> Dear Mr. Worthington,
>
> I was greatly impressed by your review in the *Booksy Weekly* of my novel *Whither If Anywhere* in which you say that my construction is lamentable, my dialogue leaden and my characters stuffed with sawdust, and advise me to give up writing and get a job in a putty-knife factory.
>
> Oddly enough, I do have a job in a putty-knife factory. I write in the evenings, and I should

hate to give it up, and I feel sure that, now that I have read your most erudite and helpful criticisms, I can correct the faults you mention and gradually improve my output until it meets with your approval. (And I need scarcely say that I would rather have the approval of Eustace Worthington than that of any other man in the world, for I have long been a sincere admirer of your brilliant work.)

I wonder if you would care to have lunch with me sometime and go further into the matter of my book and its many defects. Shall we say the Colony some day next week?

Yours faithfully,
G. G. SIMMONS

P.S. What an excellent article that was of yours in the *Police Gazette* some weeks ago on "The Disintegration of Reality in the Interest of the Syncretic Principle." I could hardly wait to see how it all came out.
P.P.S. Are you fond of caviar?
P.P.SS. I will see if I can get the Duke of Windsor to come along. I know how much he would like to meet you.

This is good and nearly always makes friends and influences people, but I confess that I prefer the other kind, the belligerent. This is possibly because the Wodehouses are notoriously hot-blooded. (It was a Wodehouse who in the year 1911 did seven days in the county jail—rather than pay a fine—for failing to abate a smoky chimney.)

Specimen B. The Belligerent

SIR:

Not "Dear Sir." Weak. And not "You louse," which is strong but a little undignified. Myself, I have sometimes used "You fatheaded fool" and once "Listen, you son of a bachelor," but I prefer "Sir."

SIR:

So you think my novel *Storm over Flatbush* would disgrace a child of three with water on the brain, do you? Who are you to start shooting off your head, you contemptible hack? If you were any good, you wouldn't be writing book reviews for a rag like the one you befoul with your idiotic contributions, the circulation of which, I happen to know, is confined exclusively to inmates of Bloomingdale and members of the proprietor's family.

Your opinion, may I add, would carry greater authority with me, did I not know, having met people who (with difficulty) tolerate your society, that you still owe your tailor for that pair of trousers he made for you in the spring of 1946 and that the lady who presides over the boardinghouse which you infest is threatening, if you don't pay six weeks' back rent soon, to throw you out on the seat of them.

Yours faithfully,

CLYDE WEATHERBEE

P.S. *Where were you on the night of June the fifteenth?*

Now that's good. That cleanses the bosom of the perilous stuff that weighs upon the heart. But don't send this kind of letter to the editor of the paper, because editors always allow the critic to shove in a reply in brackets at the end of it, thus giving him the last word.

2

As a matter of fact, though, I was quite pleased to come across that slam at Jeeves, for I have felt for some time that something should be done to restore vigor and vitality to literary criticism, and this seemed to show that here and there traces of the old rugged spirit still lingered. Too many critics today are gentle souls who would not harm so much as a minor poet. But when I was a young man they lived on raw meat, and an author who published a book did so at his own risk. If he got by without severe contusions of his self-respect, he knew that he must be pretty good. And if the reception of his first novel left him feeling as if he had been drawn through a wringer or forcibly unclothed in public, that was an excellent thing for his art. It put him on his toes. If he had the right stuff in him, he persevered. If he hadn't, he gave it up.

But nowadays reviewers are all sweetness and light, and the question "Have you read any good books lately?" is one which it is impossible to answer, for there are no good books now—only superb books, astounding books, richly rewarding books, vitally significant books and books which we are not ashamed to say brought tears to our eyes.

Some people (who ought to blush for themselves) say that the reason for this tidal wave of amiability is the fact that reviewers today are all novelists themselves, and this tempers their acerbity. Old Bill, they argue, who does the literary page of *The Scrutineer*, is not going to jump on Old Joe's *Sundered Souls* when he knows that his own *Through a Mist Darkly* is coming out next week and that Joe does the book column in *The Spokesman*.

This, of course, is not so. Nobody who really knows reviewers and their flaming integrity would believe it for a moment. It is with genuine surprise that William, having added *Sundered Souls* to the list of the world's masterpieces, finds that Joseph, a week later, has done the same to *Through a Mist Darkly*. An odd coincidence, he feels.

No, the whole trouble is that critics today, with the exception of a few of the younger set who have an unpleasant downy growth alongside the ears, are all clean-shaven, whereas those of a more virile age let the jungle in. The Edinburgh reviewers were beavers to a man, and everybody knows how bitter they were.

Whether they were bitter because they had beards or grew beards because they were bitter is beside the point. The fact remains that all the great literary rows you read about were between men who looked like English sheep dogs. They used to get into fights in clubs and roll about on

the floor, clawing at each other's beards, thereby increasing the gaiety of nations more than somewhat.

The connection between superfluous hair and caustic criticism is not hard to understand. There is probably nothing which so soothes a man and puts him in a frame of mind to see only good in everything as a nice clean shave. He feels his smooth, pink cheeks, and the milk of human kindness begins to gurgle within him. "What a day!" he says, as he looks out of window. "What eggs! What bacon!" he says, as he starts his breakfast. And, if he is a literary critic, "What a book!" he feels as he leafs through the pages of the latest ghastly effort of some author who ought to be selling coals instead of writing novels. And with tears dripping from the end of his nose he records this opinion in his column.

But let a man omit to shave, even for a single day, and mark the result. He feels hot and scrubby. Within twelve hours his outlook has become jaundiced and captious. If his interests lie in the direction of politics, he goes out and throws a bomb at someone. If he is an employer of labor, he starts a lockout. If he is a critic, he sits down to write his criticism with the determination that by the time he has finished the author will know he has been in a fight.

You have only to look about you to appreciate the truth of this. All whiskered things are testy and short-tempered—pumas, wildcats, the late Karl Marx and, in the mating season, shrimps. Would Ben Jonson have knifed a man on account of some literary disagreement if he had not been bearded to the eyebrows? Can you imagine a nation of spruce, clean-shaven Bolsheviks, smelling of Mennen's skin lotion? There is only one thing to be done. We must go back to whiskers. And there must be no half-measures.

It is not enough to have a beard like Rex Stout's, which, though technically a beard, is not bushy enough to sour the natural kindliness of his disposition. We must have the old Assyrian grogans, the great, cascading, spade-shaped things the old Victorians grew—whether under glass or not has never been ascertained. Then we shall begin to get somewhere.

I realize that I shall suffer from the change. There will be no more of those eulogies of my work like "8 by 10½, 315 pp.," which I have been pasting into my scrapbook for so many years. But I am prepared to sacrifice myself for the sake of literature, and I know that a general outcropping of spinach among critics would raise the whole standard of writing.

A young author would think twice before starting his introspective novel of adolescence if he knew that it would be handed over for review to somebody who looked like Wilkie Collins at the age of sixteen. Nervous women would stop writing altogether, and what a break that would be for the reading public. The only novelists who would carry on would be the small, select group of tough eggs who had what it takes.

And it is useless for the critics to protest their inability to fall in with the idea. It is perfectly easy to grow whiskers. There used to be a whiskered all-in wrestler called Man Mountain Dean. He did it. Are our reviewers going to tell me that they are inferior in will power and determination to an all-in wrestler?

Tush!

If I have seemed to speak warmly on this subject, it is because it is one on which I hold very strong views. I have embodied these in a lyric which I am sure you will all want to hear. It is supposed to be sung by a small bearded man who goes to a party and they ask him to sing, and he says Oh, I can't, and they say Oh, do, and he says the only thing he can sing is a song about whiskers, so they say All right, sing a song about whiskers. And he clears his throat and says "Mi-mi-mi" a couple of times in an undertone, and begins:

The world is in a mess today,
Damn sight worse than yesterday,
And getting a whole lot worser right along.
It's time that some clear-thinking guy
Got up and told the reason why
America has started going wrong.
If laws are broke and homes are wrecked,
It's only what you might expect
With all the fellows shaving all the time.
Yes, sir, the moment you begin
To crop the fungus from the chin
You're headed for a life of sin
And crime.

What this country needs is men with whiskers
Like the men of an earlier date.
They were never heels and loafers
And they looked like busted sofas
Or excelsior in a crate.
Don't forget it was men with whiskers
Who founded our New Yorks, Detroits and San
  Franciskers.
What this country needs is men with whiskers
Like the men who made her great.

The pioneers were hairy men,
Reckless devil-may-care-y men,

Who wouldn't have used a razor on a bet.
For each had sworn a solemn oath
He'd never prune the undergrowth;
Their motto was "To hell with King Gillette!"
And when they met on country walks
Wild Cherokees with tomahawks,
I'll say those boys were glad they hadn't shaved.
When cornered by a redskin band,
With things not going quite as planned,
They hid inside their whiskers and
Were saved.

What this country needs is men with whiskers,
For the whisker always wins.
Be it war or golf or tennis
We shall fear no foeman's menace
With alfalfa on our chins.
Whitman's verse, there is none to match it,
But you couldn't see his face unless you used a hatchet.
What this country needs is men with whiskers
Out where the best begins.

What this country needs is men with whiskers
Like the men of Lincoln's day.
At the Wilderness and Shiloh
They laid many a doughty guy low,
They were heroes in the fray.
Theirs is fame that can never die out,
And if you touched their beards, a couple of birds
  would fly out,
So let's raise the slogan of "Back to whiskers!"
And three cheers for the U.S.A.

3

As regards my stressing the butler note too determinedly in my writing, the critics are probably correct.

"Why is it," asks one of them in a thoughtful passage, "that Wodehouse writes so much about butlers? There must be an explanation. This squareshooter would not do it without some excellent reason."

Well, I'll tell you. Butlers have always fascinated me. As a child, I was raised on the fringe of the butler belt; as a young man I was a prominent pest at houses where butlers were maintained; and later I employed butlers; so it might be said that I have never really gone off the butler standard. And all through the years these men have piqued my curiosity. Mystery hangs about them like a nimbus. How do they get that way? What do they think about? Where do they go on their evenings off? Why do they always wear derby hats? And why are they called butlers? If the word is a corruption of bottlers, it is surely a misnomer. A butler does not bottle. He unbottles.

Though not today. Very little unbottling has taken place since the social revolution set in in England. For forty years and more I have omitted no word or act to keep butlers in the forefront of public thought, and now they have ceased to be. I have been goggled at by my last butler. Makes one sort of sad, that.

It is possible that at this point you will try to bring the

roses back to my cheeks by mentioning a recent case in the London courts where a young peer was charged with biting a lady friend in the leg and much of the evidence was supplied by "the butler." I read about that too, and it cheered me up for a moment. But only for a moment. I told myself cynically that this "butler" was probably just another of those modern makeshifts. No doubt in many English homes there is still buttling of a sort going on, but it is done by ex-batmen, promoted odd-job boys and so forth, callow youngsters not to be ranked as butlers by one who, like myself, was around and about in London in 1903 and saw the real thing. Butlers? These chinless children? Faugh, if you will permit me the expression.

I have an English friend who has a butler, and I was congratulating him on this the last time we met. He listened to me, I thought, rather moodily. "Yes," he said when I had finished, "Murgatroyd is all right, I suppose. Does his work well and all that sort of thing. But," he added with a sigh, "I wish I could break him of that habit of his of sliding down the banisters."

The real, crusted, vintage butler passed away with Edward the Seventh. One tried one's best to pretend that the Georgian Age had changed nothing, but it had. The post-First-World-War butler was a mere synthetic substitute for the ones we used to know. When we old dodderers speak of butlers, we are thinking of what used to lurk behind the front doors of Mayfair at the turn of the century.

Those were the days of what—because they took place

late in the afternoon—were known as "morning calls." Somewhere around five o'clock one would put on the old frock coat (with the white piping inside the vest), polish up the old top hat (a drop of stout helped the gloss), slide a glove over one's left hand (you carried the other one) and go out and pay morning calls. You mounted the steps of some stately home, you pulled the bell, and suddenly the door opened and there stood an august figure, weighing two hundred and thirty pounds or so on the hoof, with mauve cheeks, three chins, supercilious lips and popping, gooseberry eyes that raked you with a forbidding stare, as if you were something the carrion crow had deposited on the doorstep. "Not at all what we have been accustomed to," those bulging eyes seemed to say.

That, at least, was the message I always read in them, due no doubt to my extreme youth and the fact, of which I never ceased to be vividly aware, that my brother's frock coat and my Cousin George's trousers did not begin to fit me. A certain anemia of the exchequer caused me in those days to go about in the discarded clothes of relatives, and it was this that once enabled me to see that rarest of all sights, a laughing butler. By the laws of their guild butlers of the Edwardian epoch were sometimes permitted a quick, short smile, provided it was sardonic, but never a guffaw. I will come back to this later. Wait for the story of the laughing butler.

My acquaintance with butlers and my awe of them started at a very early age. My father being a judge in Hong

Kong, my parents were abroad most of the time when I was in the knickerbocker stage, and during my school vacations I was passed from aunt to aunt. A certain number of these aunts were the wives of clergymen, which meant official calls at the local great house, and when they paid these calls they took me along. Why, I have never been able to understand. Even at the age of ten I was a social bust, contributing little or nothing to the conversation. The thing generally ended in my hostess smiling one of those painful smiles and suggesting that it would be nice for your little nephew to go and have tea in the Servants Hall.

And she was right. I loved it. My mind today is fragrant with memories of kindly footmen and vivacious parlormaids. In their society I ceased to be shy and kidded back and forth with the best of them. The life and soul of the party they will probably describe me as, when they write their autobiographies. But these good times never lasted. Sooner or later in would come the butler, like the monstrous crow in *Through the Looking Glass,* and the quips would die on our lips. "The young gentleman is wanted," he would say morosely, and the young gentleman would shamble out, feeling like $.30.

Eventually I reached the age when the hair whitens, the waistline expands and the terrors of youth leave us. The turning point came when I realized one morning that, while I was on the verge of fifty, my butler was a mere kid of forty-six. It altered the whole situation. One likes to unbend with one's juniors, and I unbent with this slip of a boy.

From tentative discussions of the weather we progressed until I was telling him what hell it was to get stuck halfway through a novel, and he was telling me of former employers of his and how the butler's cross is that he has to stand behind Mr. Big's chair night after night and listen to the funny noise he makes over his soup. You serve the soup and stand back and clench your hands. "Now comes the funny noise," you say to yourself. Night after night after night. This explains what in my youth had always puzzled me, the universal gloom of butlers.

Only once—here comes that story I was speaking of—have I heard a butler laugh. On a certain night in the year 1903, when I had been invited to dinner at a rather more stately home than usual and, owing to the friend who has appeared in some of my stories under the name of Ukridge having borrowed my dress clothes without telling me, I had to attend the function in a primitive suit of soup-and-fish bequeathed to me by my Uncle Hugh, a man who stood six feet four and weighed in the neighborhood of three hundred pounds.

Even as I dressed, the things seemed roomy. It was not, however, until the fish course that I realized how roomy they were, when, glancing down, I suddenly observed the trousers mounting like a rising tide over my shirt front. I pushed them back, but I knew I was fighting a losing battle. I was up against the same trouble that bothered King Canute. Eventually, when I was helping myself to potatoes and was off my guard, the tide swept up as far as my white tie, and it was then that Yates or Bates or Fotheringay or whatever his name was uttered a sound like a bursting paper bag and hurried from the room with his hand over his mouth, squaring himself with his guild later, I believe, by saying that he had had some kind of fit. It was an unpleasant experience and one that clouded my life through most of the period 1903–4–5, but it is something to be able to tell my grandchildren that I once saw a butler laugh.

Among other things which contributed to make butlers gloomy was the fact that so many of their employers were sparkling raconteurs. Only a butler, my butler said, can realize what it means to a butler to be wedged against the sideboard and unable to escape and to watch his employer working the conversation around to the point where he will be able to tell that good story of his which he, the butler, has heard so often before. It was when my butler mentioned this, with a kindly word of commendation to me for never having said anything even remotely clever or entertaining since he had entered my service, that I at last found myself understanding the inwardness of a rather peculiar episode of my early manhood.

A mutual friend had taken me to lunch at the house of W. S. (Savoy Operas) Gilbert just outside London, and midway through the meal the great man began to tell a story. It was one of those very long, deceptively dull stories where you make the build-up as tedious as you can and pause before you reach the point, so as to stun the audience with the unexpected snaperoo. In other words, a story which is pretty awful till the last line, when everything becomes joy and jollity.

Well, sir, there was Sir William Schwenck Gilbert telling this long story, and there was I, a pie-faced lad of twenty-two in my brother's frock coat and my Cousin George's trousers, drinking it respectfully in. It did not seem to me very funny, but I knew it must be because this was W. S. Gilbert telling it, so when the pause before the punch line came, I laughed.

I had rather an individual laugh in those days, something like the explosion of a gas main. Infectious, I suppose you would call it, for the other guests, seeming a little puzzled, as if they had expected something with rather more point from the author of *The Mikado*, also laughed politely, and conversation became general. And it was at this juncture that I caught mine host's eye.

I shall always remember the glare of pure hatred which I saw in it. If you have seen photographs of Gilbert, you will be aware that even when in repose his face was inclined to be formidable and his eye not the sort of eye you would willingly catch. And now his face was far from being in repose. His eyes, beneath their beetling brows, seared my very soul. In order to get away from them, I averted my gaze and found myself encountering that of the butler. His eyes were shining with a doglike devotion. For some reason which I was unable to understand, I appeared to have made his day. I know now what that reason was. I suppose he had heard that story build up like a glacier and rumble to its conclusion at least twenty times, probably more, and I had killed it.

And now Gilbert has gone to his rest, and his butler has gone to his rest, and all the other butlers of those great days have gone to their rests. Time, like an ever-rolling stream, bears all its sons away, and even the English butler has not been immune. He has joined the Great Auk, the passenger pigeon and the snows of yesterday in limbo.

But I like to think that we shall meet beyond the river. I cannot believe that this separation will endure forever. I tell myself that when the ninth Earl of Emsworth, who is now, I suppose, rubbing along at Blandings Castle with the assistance of a charwoman, finally hands in his dinner pail after his long and pleasant life, the first thing he will hear as he settles himself on his cloud will be the fruity voice of Beach, his faithful butler, saying "Nectar or ambrosia, m'lord?"

"Eh? Oh, hullo, Beach. I say, Beach, what's this dashed thing?"

"A harp, m'lord."

"What am I supposed to do with it?"

"Play on it, m'lord."

"Eh? Play on it? Oh, you mean *play* on it. Like Harpo Marx, you mean?"

"Precisely, m'lord."

"Most extraordinary."

"Yes, m'lord."

"Is everybody doing it?"

"Yes, m'lord."

"My sister Constance? My brother Galahad? Sir Gregory Parsloe? Everybody?"

"Yes, m'lord."

"Oh? Sounds odd to me. Still, if you say so. Give me your A, Beach."

"Very good, m'lord."

My Iron Resolve to Take Ish

1

I HAVE TOLD the story of my early struggles, showing how by the simple process of calling myself Pelham Grenville Wodehouse I was enabled to rise on stepping stones of my dead self to higher things and get into the chips, and here, I suppose, if I really knew how to write an autobiography, I would describe in pitiless detail what I did after that. But though it will probably mean my getting drummed out of the Autobiographers' Guild and having my buttons—coat buttons only, let us hope—snipped off in a hollow square, I shall refrain. To my mind there is nothing so soporific as an author's account of his career after he has become established. As one of the good gray poets once said: Of all sad words by plane or boat, the saddest are these—"And then I wrote . . ."

I have known novelists, when relating the story of their lives, to give not only a complete list of their novels but the plots of many of them. Brutal, I call it. Far better, when one feels an autobiography coming on, to remember the splendid words of Mr. Glen Johns of Fort Erie, Ontario, on the occasion of his winning the raw-egg-eating championship of Canada last spring—ah, Fort Erie, Ontario, in the springtime!—by eating twenty-four raw eggs in fourteen minutes.

A thing I never understand, when I read an item like that in the paper, is how these fellows do it. I mean, you take me. I have built up a nice little conservative business over the years, and there is no mystery about my beginnings. You can trace my progress step by step. But how does a man so shape himself that he becomes able to eat twenty-four raw eggs in fourteen minutes?

One feels the same thing about performers at the circus. How did the man who dives through a hole in the roof into a small tank first get the impulse? One pictures him studying peacefully for the Church, without a thought in his mind of any other walk in life, when suddenly, as he sits poring over his theological books, a voice whispers in his ear. "This is all very well," says the voice, "but what you were really intended to do was to dive through holes in the roof into tanks. Do not stifle your individuality. Remember the parable of the talents." And he throws away his books and goes out to see an agent. Some sort of spiritual revelation like this no doubt happened to Mr. Johns.

But I was going to tell you about those splendid words he spoke. Interviewed after the twenty-fourth egg and asked how he did it, he replied: "I ate twenty-one eggs in twelve minutes, and then I ate another three, making twenty-four in all."

"No, no, I mean how did you *start*?"

"With the first egg . . . Call it Egg A or (1). I ate that egg, then I ate another egg, then I ate another egg, then I ate another egg, then I ate another egg, then I ate another egg, then I ate another egg, then . . ."

Substitute "wrote" for "ate" and "book" for "egg," and an author has said everything that needs to be said.

For the benefit of the small minority who are interested in statistics I will state briefly that since 1902 I have produced ten books for boys, one book for children, forty-three novels, three hundred and fifteen short stories and have been author or part author of sixteen plays and have written the lyrics for twenty-two musical comedies. Then there is the matter of light verse. I have written more light verse than you would think possible. In the six years that I was doing the "By the Way" column on the *Globe* I had to write a set of verses every morning between 10:00 and 11:30 in addition to the paragraphs, and I suppose there is no man alive more qualified to turn out one of those You Too Can

Croon in June pieces which you see in literary papers. But it was only recently that I became a serious poet.

They do ask the darnedest questions on television. There is a thing on Sunday nights called Elder Wise Men, and the elderly sage they got hold of the other evening was John Hall Wheelock, the man who wrote a poem about having a black panther caged within his breast (than which I can imagine nothing more disturbing for anyone of settled habits and a liking for the quiet life).

"Tell me, Mr. Wheelock," said the interviewer—who was something special in the way of TV interviewers, few of whom have any peers when it comes to asking the fatuous question—"could you have helped being a poet?"

The implication being, one presumes, that he felt that Mr. Wheelock hadn't *tried*. He could have pulled up in time if he had had the right stuff in him, but he adopted a weak policy of drift and *laissez-faire*, and the next thing he knew he was writing about panthers caged within his breast.

"I don't believe I could," said Mr. Wheelock, and one pictures the interviewer clicking his tongue censoriously.

But I doubt that the thing is always deliberate. Many who become poets are more to be pitied than censured. What happens is that they are lured on the downward path by the fatal fascination of the limerick form. It is so terribly easy to compose the first two lines of a limerick and, that done, the subject finds it impossible to stop. (Compare the case of the tiger cub which, at first satisfied with a bowl of milk, goes in strictly for blood after tasting its initial coolie.) And the difficulty of finding a last line discourages these men from sticking to limericks, which would be fairly harmless. So they take the easier way and write serious poetry. It was after they had scribbled down on the back of a bill of fare at the Mermaid Tavern

There was a young lady (Egyptian)
Who merits a word of description

that Shakespeare, Bacon, Marlowe and the Earl of Oxford realized that the rhyme scheme was too tough.

"Bipshion?" suggested Bacon. (He would.)

"What do you mean, bipshion?" said Marlowe irritably. "There isn't such a word."

"Hips on?"

"Doesn't rhyme."

"I seem to have heard people talking of having conniption fits," said Shakespeare diffidently. "How about 'And she suffered from fits (viz., conniption)'? Just a suggestion."

"And as rotten a one as I ever heard," snapped Marlowe.

"Oh, hell," said the Earl of Oxford. (These peers express themselves strongly.) "Let's turn it into a play."

And they wrote *Antony and Cleopatra.*

A similar thing happened with Tennyson's

There was a young fellow named Artie
Who was always the life of the party.

This subsequently became *Idylls of the King.*

My own case is rather interesting. As I say, I had never written anything but light, frivolous verse, but I happened one Sunday morning to be skimming through my *New York Times*—for though well stricken in years, I can still lift my Sunday *New York Times*—and as I turned to the correspondence page of the book section I suddenly quivered in every limb. It was as though I had been slapped between the eyes with a wet fish.

I don't know if you know the correspondence page of the book section of the Sunday *New York Times*. It consists of heated letters denouncing opinions expressed in letters of the previous week, and what had attracted my attention was one that began:

SIR:

I take issue with Percy G. Swisher . . .

I would like my readers to try repeating those words to themselves. I think they will find that after a few minutes their haunting beauty grips them as it gripped me. I felt, and I have no doubt they will feel, that only poetry—and the finest poetry—could do justice to the theme. In a trice I was at my desk with the old pipe drawing well and a pot of black coffee at my elbow, and in another trice—if not sooner—I was well into my first serious poem. (The stuff seemed just to pour out.)

It would be a dirty trick, after getting you all worked up

like this, to withhold it from you, and I do not propose to do so. It ran:

The day, I recall, was a spring one,
Not hot and oppressive, though warm,
The sort of a day apt to bring one
Right up to the top of one's form.
So when a kind friend and well-wisher
Said "Don't just sit dreaming there, kid.
Take issue with Percy G. Swisher,"
I replied "Yes, I will." And I did.

I felt rather sorry for Percy.
I hated to crush the poor fish.
But no inclination to mercy
Could shake my resolve to take ish.
You can't be a competent isher,
If from thoughts of the rough stuff you wince.
I took issue with Percy G. Swisher.
He's never been quite the same since.

So though low in the world's estimation,
A bit of a washout, in short,
I have always this one consolation:
I tell myself, "Courage, old sport!
There are others more gifted and risher
And plenty more beautiful, BUT
You took issue with Percy G. Swisher,
So you might be much more of a mutt."

From there to writing "Excelsior" and "The Boy Stood on the Burning Deck" was but a step.

2

There was a millionaire in one of George Ade's *Fables* who, having devoted a long life to an unceasing struggle to amass his millions, looked up from his deathbed and said plaintively, "And now, perhaps, somebody will kindly tell me what it has all been about." I get that feeling sometimes. Couldn't I, I ask myself, have skipped one or two of those works of mine and gone off and played golf without hurting English literature or jeopardizing my financial position? Take, for instance, a book I wrote in 1909 called *The Swoop,* a skit on the invasion-of-England stories which were so prevalent then. I wrote the whole twenty-five thousand words of it in five days and nearly expired, and, selling at a shilling, it brought me in royalties of £9.14.6. Was it worth the trouble and anguish?

I'm glad I asked myself that. Yes, it was, for I had a great deal of fun writing it. I have had a great deal of fun—one-sided, possibly—writing all my books. Doctor Johnson once said that nobody but a blockhead ever wrote except for money. I should think it extremely improbable that anyone ever wrote anything simply for money. What makes a writer write is that he likes writing. How about the people who write letters to the papers saying they have heard the cuckoo, Doc? Are you telling me they do it for money? You're crazy, Johnson. They do it because they have something to say which they must get out of their systems. They are the people Walter Pater had in mind when he spoke of "burning with a hard gemlike flame."

Although it is many years since I myself gave up writing letters to the papers, I still keep in close touch with the correspondence columns of the English journals, and it is a source of considerable pain to me to note today what appears to be a conspiracy of silence with regard to the cuckoo, better known possibly to some of my readers as the *Cuculus canorus*. I allude to the feathered friend which puzzled the poet Wordsworth so much. "O Cuckoo! shall I call thee Bird, Or but a wandering Voice?" he used to say, and I don't believe he ever did get straight about it.

In my young days in England the cuckoo was big stuff. Thousands hung upon its lightest word. The great thing, of course, was to be the first to hear it, for there was no surer way of getting your letter printed.

Virtually all the men at the top of the profession—Verb Sap, Pro Bono Publico, Fiat Justitia, and the like—had started their careers by hearing the first cuckoo and getting the story off to the paper while it was hot. It was the recognized *point d'appui* for the young writer.

"My boy," I remember Fiat Justitia saying to me once after he had been kind enough to read some of my unpublished material, "don't let editorial rejections discourage you. Where you have gone wrong is in writing about social trends and the political situation. You must not try to run before you can walk. Begin, like all the great masters, with the cuckoo. And be careful that it is a cuckoo. I knew a man who wrote to his daily paper saying that he had heard the first reed-warbler, and the letter was suppressed because it would have given offense to certain powerful vested interests."

But how changed are conditions today. My attention has been drawn to a letter in one of the London Sunday papers:

Sir:

If the hypothesis be accepted without undue dogmatism in the present rudimentary state of our knowledge that brain is merely the instrument of mind and not its source, the terms soul and spirit could plausibly be regarded as redundant.

Pretty poor stuff. Not a word about hearing the cuckoo, which could have been brought in perfectly neatly in a hundred ways.

Before I broke into the game I used to think of the men who had their attention drawn as unworldly dreamers living in some ivory tower, busy perhaps on a monumental history of the Ming dynasty or something of that sort and never seeing the papers. But when I became a correspondent myself and joined the well-known Fleet Street club, The Twelve Jolly Letter-Writers, I found I had been mistaken. Far from being dreamers, the "My-attention-has-been-drawn" fellows were the big men of the profession, the topnotchers.

You started at the bottom of the ladder with:

Sir:

I heard the cuckoo yesterday . . .

then after some years rose to a position where you said:

SIR:

The cuckoo is with us once again, its liquid notes ringing through the countryside. Yesterday . . .

and finally, when the moment had come, you had your attention drawn.

There was, as I recollect it, no formal promotion from the ranks, no ceremony of initiation or anything like that. One just sensed when the time was ripe for one to become an A.D., like an English barrister, who has built up a large practice as what is known in legal circles as a Junior, when he decides that the time is ripe for him to become a Queen's Counsel, or, as the expression is, to "take silk."

I inadvertently caused something of a flutter in the club, I remember, soon after I had taken silk, and got hauled over the coals by that splendid old veteran Mother of Six (Oswaldtwistle).

"Gussie," he said to me one morning—I was writing under the name of Disgusted Taxpayer in those days, "I have a bone to pick with you. My attention has been drawn to a letter of yours in the *Daily Telegraph* in which you say that your attention has been called to something."

"What's wrong with called?" I said. I was young and headstrong then.

"It is not done," he replied coldly. "Attentions are not called, they are drawn. Otherwise, why would Tennyson in his well-known poem have written:

Tomorrow'll be the happiest time of all the glad new year.
Of all the glad new year, Mother, the maddest merriest day,
For my attention has been drawn to a statement in the press that I'm to be Queen of the May, Mother, I'm to be Queen of the May.

I never made that mistake again.

3

Returning to Doctor Johnson, I am sorry I had to put him in his place like that and make such a monkey of him. I ought to have remembered that when he said that silly thing about writing for money he was not feeling quite himself. He was all hot and cross because of the Lord Chesterfield business. You probably remember the circumstances. He had wanted Lord Chesterfield to be his patron, and had been turned down like a bedspread. No wonder he was in ugly mood.

In the days when I was hammering out stories for the pulps and trying not to listen to the soft whining of the wolf outside the door I often used to think how wonderful it would be if the patron system of the eighteenth century could be revived. None of that nonsense then of submitting your novel to a cold-eyed publisher and having to listen to him moaning about the growing cost of paper and regretting the impossibility under existing conditions of springing anything in the nature of an advance. All you had to do was to run over the roster of the peerage and select your patron.

You wanted somebody fairly weak in the head, but practically all members of the peerage in those happy days were weak in the head and, there being no income tax or surtax then, they could fling you purses of gold without feeling it. Probably some kindly friend put you on to the right man. "Try young Sangazure," he said. "I know the nurse who dropped him on his head when a baby. Give him the old oil and it's a cinch. Don't forget to say 'My lord' and 'Your lordship' all the time. They love it."

I have never been able quite to understand what were the actual preliminaries. I imagine that you waited till your prospect had written a poem—and this was bound to happen sooner or later—and then you hung around in his anteroom till you were eventually admitted to the presence. You found your man lying on a sofa reading the eighteenth-century equivalent of *Captain Billy's Whizz Bang*, and when he said "Yes?" or "Well?" or "Who on earth let *you* in?" you explained that you had merely come to look at him. "No, don't move, my lord," you said. "And don't speak for a moment. Let me just gaze at your lordship." You wanted, you said, to feast your eyes on the noble brow from which had proceeded that "Ode to Spring."

The effect was instantaneous.

"Oh, I say, really?" said the member of the peerage, softening visibly and drawing a pattern on the carpet with his left toe.

"You really liked the little thing, what?"

"*Liked* it, my lord! It knocked me flatter than a griddle

cake, my lord. That bit at the beginning, 'Er, Spring, you perfectly priceless old thing.' Some spin on the ball there, my lord. However did your lordship do it?"

"Oh, just thought of it, you know, and sloshed it down as it were. Just thought of it and sloshed it down, if you see what I mean."

"Genius! Genius! Do you work regular hours, my lord, or does your lordship wait for inspiration?"

"W. for i. mostly. But tell me. You seem a knowledgeable sort of bloke. Do you write yourself by any chance? I mean write and all that sort of rot, what?"

"Why, yes, my lord, I am a writer, my lord. Not in your lordship's class, of course, but I do scribble a bit."

"Make a good thing out of it?"

"So far no, my lord. You see, to get anywhere these days, my lord, you have to have a patron, and patrons don't grow on every bush, my lord. How did that thing of your lordship's go? Ah, yes. 'Oh Spring, oh Spring, oh glorious Spring, when cuckoos sing like anything.' Your lordship certainly gave that one the works."

"Yes, not baddish, was it? Rather goodish, what, what? I say, look here, here's a thought. How about me being your patron?"

"Your lordship's condescension overwhelms me."

"Right ho, then, that's all fixed up. Tell my major-domo as you go out to fling you a purse of gold."

4

Recently I have seemed to detect welcome signs indicating that the patron is coming back. I wrote a piece the other day about being in the telephone book, in which I gave my telephone number.

"In the life of every man living in New York and subscribing to the New York Telephone service" (I wrote) "there comes a moment when he has to face a problem squarely and make a decision. Shall he—or, alternatively, shall he not—have his name in the book? There is no middle course. Either you are in the book or you aren't. I am in myself. I suppose it was wanting to have something good to read in the long winter evenings that made me do it. For unquestionably it reads well.

"Wodehouse P G 1000 PkAv . . . BUtrfld 8-7598. Much better, it seems to me—zippier is perhaps the word I want—than Wodczaika Theo 279 Riv Dr . . . ACdmy 2-6098, which comes immediately before it, and Wodilly Selma 577 Grand . . . CAnl 6-0099, which comes immediately after. Both are good enough in their way, but they are not Wodehouse P G 1000 PkAv . . . BUtrfld 8-7598. In moods of depression I often turn to the well-thumbed page, and it always puts new heart in me. 'Wodehouse P G,' I say to myself. '1000PkAv,' I say to myself. 'BUtrfld 8-7598,' I say to myself. 'Pretty good, pretty good.' "

Well, for weeks after the article had appeared no day passed without two or three people calling up to ask if that really was my telephone number. One of them called all the way from Pasadena, California. He said—this seems almost inconceivable, but I am quoting him verbatim—he said he thought my books were God-awful and he couldn't read another of them if you paid him, but he did enjoy my articles and would I like a Russell Flint print of a nude sit-ing on the banks of the Loire. I said I would—you can't have too many nudes about the home—and it now hangs over my desk. And the point I am making is this: Whatever we may think of a man who does not appreciate my books, we must applaud what is unquestionably the right spirit. We authors live, of course, solely for our Art, but we can always do with a little something on the side, and here, unless I am mistaken, we have the old patron system coming into its own again. It should, in my opinion, be encouraged.

If any other members of my public feel like subsidizing me, what I need particularly at the moment are:

Golf Balls
Tobacco
A Cadillac
Dog Food Suitable for
(a) A Foxhound
(b) A Pekinese
Cat Food Suitable for
A Cat
and
Diamond Necklace Suitable for
A Wife

I could also do with a case of champagne and some warm winter woolies. And a few shares of United States Steel would not hurt.

Contributions should be addressed to me at Blandings Castle, Basket Neck Lane, Remsenburg, Long Island, New York.

The Slave of a Bad Habit

1

For I am living in the country now. Call me up at BU 8-7598 as of even date, and you will be answered by Mignon G. Eberhart, the mystery writer, who has taken on the old duplex pnthse apt., unless she's changed the number.

I loved that duplex pnthse apt, but—or, as we fellows in the book say, BUt—I am not sorry to have moved. Being in the book, I got publicity of the right sort and my winter evening reading was all arranged for, but the trouble was that when people, curled up in the old armchair with the New York Telephone Directory, saw

Wodehouse P G 1000 Pk Ave........BUtrfld 8-7598

it put ideas into their heads. Briefly, I had become, especially around Christmas time, a sitting duck for every toucher on the island of Manhattan, and it was rarely that a morning passed without my hearing a breezy voice on the telephone.

"Mr. Wodehouse?"

"Speaking."

"Is that Mr. Wodehouse?"

"In person."

"Well, well, well! Well, well, well, well, *well*! How are you, P. G., how *are* you? Fine? Fine! No colds, coughs or rheumatic ailments? Splendid. That's wonderful. This is the Rev. Cyril Twombley. You won't know my name, but I am one of your greatest fans and I simply couldn't resist the urge to call you up and tell you how much I love your books. I think I've read every line you've written. Great stuff, P. G., great stuff. Jeeves, eh? Ha ha ha ha ha!"

Well, by my halidom, I would be saying to myself by this time, this is extremely gratifying. One is above any petty caring for praise or blame, of course, but still it is nice to feel that one's efforts are appreciated. Furthermore—though one is too spiritual to give much thought to that—a man as enthusiastic as this will surely buy a copy of that book of ours that is coming out next month, which means fifty-two and a half cents in royalties in our kick, and may quite possibly give copies to his friends. (Five friends? Ten friends? Better be on the safe side and call it five. Well, that is $2.62 or thereabouts, and you can buy a lot of tobacco for $2.62.)

But hark, he is proceeding.

"That was why I had to call you, P. G., old top. I just wanted to tell you what pleasure you have given me, and I am sure a great number of other people . . . and—oh, yes—there was one other thing. Our church is getting up a Christmas bazaar and we are hoping you will . . ."

In theory the unlisted subscriber avoids all this. If you try to get a number that is not in the book, Information pins your ears back good and proper.

"Sorrrrrrr-eeeeeee, we are not allowed to give out that numbah," says Information.

But the catch is, the unlisted boys tell me, that you keep giving it out yourself to casual acquaintances who write it down and give it to their casual acquaintances who write it down and . . . but you get the idea. Pretty soon it is public property. Russell Maloney, dealing with this subject, mentions an unlisted friend of his who, totting up the score after a certain period of time, found that his number was in the possession of eleven girls he no longer liked any more, fifty-six he had never liked, a former business associate who was suing him at the moment, a discarded masseur, three upholsterers who had made estimates for covering a sofa, and an unidentified alcoholic who called up at regular intervals and always between the hours of three and four in the morning.

To another point which Mr. Maloney brought up I never

paid much attention. He thought that by being in the book you became a social outcast, scorned and sneered at by the swells who had unlisted numbers, the inference being that you couldn't be very hot if you weren't important enough to keep your number a secret confined to a small private circle.

It may be so. Nevertheless, during the seven years I was at the duplex pnthse apt I continued to instruct the brass hats of the system to publish my telephone number. A fig, I felt, for the snobs who would look down on me. What was good enough for the AAAAAAAABBEE Moving & Storage Co and for the Zzyzzy Ztamp Ztudioz Co was good enough for me.

Still, it is probably just as well that I bought this Long Island estate and became Squire Wodehouse and got away from it all.

2

There are things, of course, that one misses when one has ceased to be part of the New York scene. One is no longer, for instance, in a position to play straight for the New York taxi driver and help him get a few well-spotted laughs. I always enjoyed doing that, though there are quite a number of people who do not. Many resent the resolute Bob Hopefulness of these public servants and listen sourly as the wisecracks come pouring back at them. They think hard thoughts of the newspapermen who for years have fostered the legend of the witty taxi driver.

"They have been exalted as a group and called brilliant conversationalists so long," says one disgruntled commentator, "that they have come to believe the stories they have read about themselves and so ham it up and babble nonsense over their shoulders whenever they have a passenger who will listen."

I am not sure that it is the newspapermen who are to blame. I think the whole thing dates back to the time when one of them, a man who liked his joke of a morning, chanced to drive Eddie Cantor one day and on the strength of his *bon mots* got enrolled on the latter's staff of gag writers. The word went around that fame and fortune awaited the hackie with a good comedy routine, and the boys buckled down to it seriously, with the result that if you take a taxi now you find yourself in the position of one of those Hollywood magnates who get acted at all the time.

You know how it is if you are a Hollywood studio boss with jobs in the pictures to give away. Never a peaceful moment. Your butler recites "Gunga Din" at you as he brings you your breakfast. Your chauffeur, learning from the grapevine that a big musical is coming along, sings "*O Sole Mio*" as he helps you into your car. You get to your office and think the worst is over, and your secretary, as she hands you your mail, goes into a quick monologue whimsically humorous for the most part but always with the tear behind the smile. And when you return home in the evening, you get the butler again, this time in imitations of popular screen favorites.

It is much the same when you take a New York cab. A taxi ride in New York is not so much a taxi ride as an audition.

"Say, mister."

"Hullo?"

"English, ain't you?"

"That's right."

"I see by the papers there's a lot of talk over there about this hydrogen bomb."

"Quite a good deal, I believe."

"Same here. Fission. That's all they talk about. Just fission. Now that's a funny thing. I can remember the time when fission was what you did in the creek with a hook and line. Hey, hey, hey."

If the newspapermen are really responsible for this sort of thing, they have much to answer for. The only poor consolation one has is the reflection that if this had been taking place on the burlesque stage one would by now have been hit over the head with a rolled-up umbrella. Still, as I say, I miss it.

Only once were my cordial relations with New York taxi drivers marred. My charioteer had opened brightly and confidently, getting some nice yaks at the expense of the police force and the street-cleaning system, and then he said:

"English, ain't you?"

"That's right."

"I see by the papers there's a lot of talk over there about this hydrogen bomb."

"Quite a good deal, I believe."

"Don't talk about much else, do they?"

"Not much."

"Now that's a funny thing. I can remember——"

"Yes," I said. "You know how it is in England. All that interests them is huntin', shootin' and fission."

He gave a startled gasp, and silence fell, lasting till we arrived at my destination. My better self had woken by now, and I gave him a fifty-cent tip, but there was no light in his somber eyes as he trousered it.The unforgivable sin had been committed. He was feeling as Danny Kaye might feel if his supporting cast started hogging the comedy. As he drove away, his head was bowed and his air that of a man who has been wounded in his finest feelings.

3

But I suppose the thing one misses most in the country is the crime wave. One got a lot of crime in New York. It seemed to be all the go. Practically everyone you met was either coming away from sticking up a bank or just setting out to stick up a bank, for these institutions have a fascination for the criminal classes, attracting them much as catnip attracts cats. A young man went into a bank the other day and asked to see the manager. Conducted into his office, he said he wanted a loan.

"Ah, yes," said the manager. "A loan, eh? Yes, yes, to be sure. And what is your occupation?"

"I stick up banks," said the young man, producing a gun.

The manager handed over $204 without collateral or argument.

But the underworld is not hidebound. It prefers banks, but it is always ready to try a sideline, realizing that a change of routine keeps a man fresh and alert. A short while before I withdrew to the country I had a visit from the police. No, nothing I had done. I was as pure as the driven snow. What these policemen wanted was to sell me a gadget designed to baffle the criminal classes when they called at the back door and knocked on it and said they were from the grocer's, delivering groceries, and then, when you let them in, stuck you up.

The cagey thing, of course, was not to let them in, and that was where you got your eight dollars' worth out of this gadget. It was a round affair with a hole and a flap and you fixed it to your back door, and when the criminal classes arrived and said they were from the grocer's, you lifted the flap and looked through the hole and said, "Oh, you are, are you? Then where are the groceries, and why are you wearing a black mask and toting around a whacking great sawn-off shotgun?" Upon which, they slunk off with horrid imprecations.

I bought the gadget, and as I attached it to the door I found myself wondering why it is worth these crime wavers' while to take so much trouble for such small results.

I am not, of course, speaking of the aristocracy of the profession who rob banks and loot the apartments of Texas millionaires. They make a nice living, their earnings being substantial and free of income tax. I mean the young fellows who waylay passers-by on dark nights. Start waylaying passers-by on dark nights, and nobody you meet ever seems to have more than $1.50 on him. Nine times out of ten he has left his wallet on the dressing table at home or turns out to be a policeman in plain clothes. I would not advise any youngster I was fond of to adopt this profession.

And apart from the meager gains the whole thing must be so embarrassing. You know how you feel when you have to accost a perfect stranger. You cough and shuffle your feet and say, "Er, excuse me." I don't see how you can begin with "This is a stick-up." It sounds so abrupt. I suppose the thing to do would be to lead up to it, sort of.

"Oh—er—excuse me, could you oblige me with a match? What a nuisance it is to run short of matches, is it not? The evenings seem to be drawing in now, don't they? Christmas will be here before we know it, will it not? Good night, sir, good night, and many thanks. Oh, by the way, before I forget. Might I trouble you to hand over your money and valuables?"

That might ease the strain a little, but nothing could ever make it pleasant for a shy man to do this sort of thing. Suppose you happen to run across somebody whose hearing is not as keen as it might be.

You say, "This is a stick-up."

He says, "Huh?"

You say, "A stick-up."

He says, "Huh?"

You say, "A stick-up. A STICK-up. S for Samuel, T for Thomas——"

He says, "I'm afraid I couldn't tell you. I'm a stranger in these parts myself."

Then what?

But the gravest peril in the path of the young stick-up man, to my mind, is the fatal tendency to get into a rut. Consider the case of one whom for convenience sake we will call The Phantom. I quote from my daily paper:

> Lazarus Koplowitz and his wife Bella live at 60 Sixth Avenue, Brooklyn, where they operate a candy store. Three times in the last month they have been robbed by the same man, who appears at the same time of day—3:15 P.M.—and threatens them with the same knife. The first time, on February 10, the unwelcome caller took $10 from Mr. Koplowitz. He returned on February 17 and took $10 from Mrs. Koplowitz.
>
> Police planted a detective in the store for some days at the calling hour, then took him away. On February 24, the man came back and took $10.

I see no future for this Phantom. He has become the slave of a habit.

Life among the Armadillos

1

WE GET NONE of that sort of thing down here at Remsenburg, but life is never dull. There is always something doing. One morning not long ago the telephone-answering executive of the New York *Herald Tribune* answered the telephone, and the caller said that his name was Sidney A. Schwartz. He lived at Riverhead, Long Island, where he kept bees.

"Ah, yes, bees," said the *Herald Tribune* man. "And how are they all?"

"They're fine," said Mr. Schwartz, "but what I called up for was to ask if you would like to have ten armadillos."

It was a strange and interesting story that he had to relate. What put the idea into his head he could not say, but one afternoon as he was looking at his bees the thought flashed into his mind—Why bees? Why not armadillos?

He knew nothing of armadillos at this time except that nobody had ever claimed that they wrote the plays of Shakespeare, but he went out and bought a couple, and it so happened that they were of opposite sexes.

Well, you know what that means in armadillo circles. All that Kinsey stuff. And when the union of two armadillos is blessed, the result is eight armadillos, sometimes more but never less. Pretty soon armadillos began to sprout in every nook and cranny of the Schwartz home. Some houses have beetles, some have mice. His had armadillos, and he soon became apprised of the drawbacks to this state of affairs. In addition to requiring large quantities of dog food, frozen horse meat, cod-liver oil and cream cheese, which dented the household budget considerably, armadillos—for reasons best known to themselves—sleep all day and come to life, like dramatic critics, only after dark. And unfortunately they are noisy and rowdy.

It was not long before *chez* Schwartz had become to all intents and purposes a night club, one of the more raffish kind, with armadillos, flushed with cream cheese, staggering about and shouting and yelling and generally ending up with a couple of ugly brawls before they turned in for the day. Pandemonium is the word that springs to the lips. It does not require much imagination to picture what it must be like with ten armadillos always around, two of them singing duets, the others forming quartets and rendering "Sweet Adeline" in close harmony. Far into the small hours, mind you.

Mr. Schwartz approached the Bronx Zoo. Would they like ten armadillos? No, said the Bronx Zoo, they wouldn't. He tried to dispose of them at sacrifice prices to a New York dealer, but again there was nothing doing. He was stuck.

And this is where I think that Mr. Schwartz shows up in a very creditable light. Where a weaker man would have gone off into a corner and sat there with his head between his hands, he acted. He had always wanted a Ph.D. degree, and here, he suddenly saw, was where he could get one. He would write a thesis on the nine-banded armadillo (*Dasypus novemcinctus*) and clean up. He divided the young armadillos into two groups, it was no good trying to do anything with the father and mother, they were too soppy to register, and—I quote the *Herald Tribune*:

> One group he made to walk incessantly upon a treadmill to the extent of three miles a day. The other he allowed to lead completely sedentary lives, undisturbed by anything except the thoughts that normally disturb armadillos in the springtime. And at the end of some weeks he found that the armadillos which had led the strenuous life were happier than the armadillos which had lain slothful and passive.

And he got his Ph.D., showing that out of evil cometh good, and that has cheered him up quite a lot, but I must confess that I find the reasoning of his thesis shaky. How does he know that the athletic armadillos were happier than the other lot? They may have been just putting a brave face on things and keeping a stiff upper lip. You can't go by an armadillo's surface manner. Many an apparently cheery armadillo without, you would say, a care in the world is really nursing a secret sorrow, sobbing into its pillow and asking itself what is the good of it all and how can it shake

off this awful depression. I should require a lot more evidence than Mr. Schwartz has submitted to convince me that the ones he thinks so chirpy are really sitting on top of the world with their hats on the side of their heads.

But what interests me chiefly in the story is not the *joie de vivre* or lack of *joie de vivre* of the armadillos but the Schwartz angle. If I say that my heart bleeds for him, that is not putting it at all too strongly. He has got his Ph.D., yes, and that in a way, I suppose, is a happy ending, but he has also got all those armadillos and more probably coming along every hour on the hour. The place must be a shambles.

Riverhead is only seven miles from where I live. I must drop over there when I can spare time and study the situation at first hand. Taking care to go in the daytime, before the cod-liver-oil corks have started to pop and the night revels have begun. One does not want unpleasantness.

2

The coming of autumn always brings a touch of sadness to the sportsman who lives in the country in America, for he finds himself at a loose end. Wasping is over. Tick-stalking is over. Worst of all, the mosquito season is a thing of the past. Nothing remains but the flies, and a big-game hunter who has looked his mosquito in the eye and made it wilt can scarcely be expected to take more than a tepid interest in flies. One likes a tang of peril with one's sport.

Compared with the mosquito, what a miserable, coddled creature a fly is. It takes three weeks to breed a new generation of flies, and even then the temperature has to be seventy degrees. A spell of cold weather, and the fly simply turns its face to the wall and packs up. How different with the mosquito. Two million dollars are spent yearly in efforts to keep mosquito eggs from hatching. Lamps, sprays and drenches without number are brought into action, and oil in tons poured on the breeding grounds. And what happens? Do they quail? Do they falter? Not by a jugful. They come out in clouds, slapping their chests and whistling through their noses, many of them with stingers at both ends.

Science has now established that the only mosquitoes that sting are the females. The boy friends like to stay at home curled up with a good book. One pictures the male mosquito as a good-natured, easy-going sort of character, not unlike Arthur Godfrey, and one can imagine him protesting feebly when the little woman starts out on a business trip.

"Oh, *no*! Not again? Are you really going out at this time of night, old girl?"

"I work better at night."

"Where are you off to now?"

"New York."

"You mean Newark?"

(The scene of the conversation is the Jersey marshes.)

"No, I don't mean Newark. I mean New York."

"You can't possibly go all the way to New York."

"Pooh."

"It's all very well to say pooh. You know as well as I do that a mosquito can only fly two hundred yards."

"I can take the Holland Tunnel."

"Costs fifty cents."

"Oh, you think of nothing but money," says the female mosquito petulantly.

And she strops her stinger on the doorstep and goes off, and probably gets squashed. Rather sad, that. Somebody's mother, you know. Still, we cannot allow ourselves to become sentimental about mosquitoes.

As an old hunter, I like the story of the general who, captured by the Chinese in Korea, relieved the monotony of imprisonment by killing mosquitoes. His record was a 522-mosquito day in 1953, but his best all-over year was 1952, when he bagged twenty-five thousand four hundred and seventy-five. The secret of success, he says, is to wait till the quarry flattens itself against the wall. The simple creature does not realize that the wall is whitewashed, and falls a ready prey to the man who, not letting a twig snap beneath his feet, sneaks up behind it with a handsomely bound copy of *The History of the Communist Party in the Soviet Union.*

Life among the Armadillos

They say 1956 is going to be a good mosquito year. Let us hope so, for there are few more stirring sights than a mosquito hunt with the men in their red coats and the hounds baying and all that sort of thing.

Meet you in the Jersey marshes.

Thin Blessings in Disguise

"WELL, from what you have been telling us, Mr. Wodehouse, it would seem that you have quite a high opinion of this America of ours."

"Extremely high. The land of the free and the home of the brave, I sometimes call it."

"Any criticisms?"

"One or two, perhaps."

"Let's have them."

"You won't be offended?"

"No, no. Go right ahead."

"Well, take, for instance, income tax."

"You view it with concern?"

"Of the deepest description."

"How well I know that feeling. There was no income tax when you first came over here, was there?"

"No. They started it in 1913. No doubt it seemed to the authorities a good idea at the time, but I think they have overdone it. It was a mistake to allow it to develop into such a popular craze. And the whole spirit has changed since those early days."

"In what way?"

"Well, take the case of a friend of mine back in 1914. He found, on going over his income tax return, that he had overpaid the Internal Revenue the sum of $1.50. He wrote a civil letter, asking for a refund, and received an equally civil reply, in which the Internal Revenue regretted the error and begged to enclose, as requested, check for $15. My friend returned the check, saying that there had been a mistake, and the authorities, more apologetic than ever, sent him another for $150. When he returned this check, they almost groveled and enclosed one for $1,500. My friend was content at this point to take his profit and retire from the game, but I still think that if he had had the vision and enterprise to carry on he could have cleaned them out. You wouldn't get anything like that happening nowadays."

"You certainly wouldn't. Of all the hard-boiled, stony-eyed, protruding-chinned lineal descendants of Jesse James who ever took the widow and the orphan by the scruff of the neck and rubbed their noses in the mud, these modern Internal Revenue thugs are the . . . But I must not allow myself to become bitter. After all, there is a bright side to the income tax."

"I have not detected it myself."

"Well, look. Say what you will, the filling up of the forms has given us all a delightful indoor game in which young and old can take part with equal enjoyment. See the family clustered around the table. There is Father, with his spectacles on, jotting down some notes on Amortization. There is Mother, leaning over his shoulder and pointing out that by taking Sec. 6248 H and putting it on top of Sub-sec. 9730 G he can claim immunity from the tax mentioned in Sec. 4537 M. And gathered about them are the children, sucking pencils and working out ways of doing down the supertax. You get the picture?"

"It rises before my eyes. 'See, Papa,' cries little Cyril gleefully, 'I note that gifts (not made as a consideration for services rendered) and money and property acquired under a will or inheritance (but the income derived from money or property received by gift, will or inheritance) are, according to Sub-sec. 2427, not subject to tax, and the way it looks to me is that you can knock off the price of the budgeregah's birdseed.' And so it goes on, each helping the other, all working together in that perfect harmony which goes to make the happy home. Nor is this all."

"I know what you are going to say. Filling in the income tax forms has kindled again all the old spirit of love and family affection. How differently nowadays the head of the house regards his wife and children. Many a man who has spent years wondering why on earth he ever linked his lot with a woman whom he has disliked from the moment they entered the Niagara Falls Hotel and a gang of boys and girls who seemed to grow more repulsive every day gratefully revises his views as he scans Schedule C. His wife may be a nuisance about the home, but she enables him to split the income. And the children. As the father looks at their hideous faces and reflects that he is entitled to knock off a nice little sum per gargoyle, the austerity of his demeanor softens and he pats them on the head and talks vaguely about ice cream for supper."

"Profoundly true. I think I must withdraw my criticism of the income tax."

"I thought you would."

"But on the subject of the New York pigeon I will speak out fearlessly, let the chips fall where they may. There are far too many pigeons in New York. Why all these pigeons? That is what I ask myself. Why?"

"Oh, well . . . You understand the facts of life, don't you? You start with a certain number of pigeons of—er—opposite sexes, and when springtime comes the male pigeon and the female pigeon, in whose bosoms there has burgeoned a feeling deeper and warmer than that of ordinary friendship . . . It's all a little delicate, of course . . . Well, to put it in a nutshell, time marches on and you get more pigeons."

" 'More' is right. I see no need for this monstrous regiment of pigeons and would like to run them all out of town . . . except Walter Pidgeon, whom I admire. But don't get me wrong. I am not a pigeonophobe. Down at Remsenburg many of my best friends are pigeons. I keep open garden for them, and you will often find half a dozen moaning if not in the immemorial elms, at least in the maple tree I bought last week from the nursery garden in Patchogue."

"I see. What you deprecate is the drift to the towns."

"Exactly. A pigeon in the country, fine. But in New York it just takes up space which could be utilized for other purposes. When I had my duplex pnthse apt at 1000 PkAv (BUtrfld 8-5029), there used to be about a thousand of them who hung around the Eighty-fifth Street entrance to the Park, sneering at passers-by and talking offensively out of the corners of their mouths. And you had to give them bread. I tried not giving them bread, but I couldn't keep it up. My nerve failed me. I knew they would fix me somehow. There are a hundred things a gang of pigeons can do to get back at those who have incurred their displeasure—gargling on the window sill at five in the morning, scaring the daylights out of you by tapping on the pane with their beaks, swooping at your face, pecking at your ankles—I couldn't risk it. It wasn't good enough."

"Appeasement, you felt, was the only course?"

"There was nothing else for it. The situation, then, until I moved to the country, was, briefly, this. Each year by the sweat of my brow I won a certain amount of bread, and this bread I would naturally have liked to reserve for the use of what for convenience' sake may be grouped under the head of 'my loved ones'—myself, my wife, my foxhound, my Pekinese and, of course, any guests who might happen to drop in. But much of it had to go to support a mob of pigeons who had never done a stroke of honest work in their lives. Playboys—every one of them. And they weren't even grateful. Slip a squirrel a bit of bread, and you get value for money. It sits up like a dog. It climbs on your arm. It does everything but give three rousing cheers. Stake a pigeon to a similar bit of bread, and what happens? Not so much as a nod of thanks. The bird just pecks at it in a condescending sort of way.

" 'Bread!' it says to the other pigeons, with a short laugh, and not a nice laugh, either. 'Stale bread! He wouldn't spring a nickel for a bag of peanuts, would he? Oh, no, not Wodehouse. Who does the man think he is? Gaspard the Miser? We'll have to fix Wodehouse.'

" 'Shall we commence on him now?' says a second pigeon.

" 'No, we must wait,' says the first pigeon. 'We can't do nothing till Martin gets here.'

"I have no doubt that if I had not fled the city and gone into hiding in Remsenburg, I should have been rubbed out by this time."

"They're tough babies."

"You're right, they're tough babies."

"Up in Washington, I see by my paper, they are hoping to chase the pigeons away from the Treasury Department building by stringing electric wires where the birds roost. William W. Parsons, Assistant Secretary of the Treasury for Administration, told a House Appropriations Subcommittee he thought it would work."

"Not a hope. It's no good, Parsons, old man. You're just a dreamer chasing rainbows, Bill, old chap. New York pigeons would scoff at such a childish device. Their feet hardened by years of mooching around Central Park, they would simply feel a pleasant tickling sensation if you touched off electric shocks under them."

"But these are Washington pigeons. They probably have not the same morale and will to win."

"No. The Treasury Department might just as well save its money. If there is one thing life has taught me, it is that there is nothing you can do about pigeons. You either have them or you don't. It is as simple as that."

"You are probably right. And is there anything else in this land of ours that you feel you wish to criticize?"

"The hurricanes."

"Ah, yes, the hurricanes. Carol and Edna and Ione and all that bunch."

"Not Ione. Ione is a nice girl. She went out to sea."

"But Carol, I believe, gave you south-shore-of-Long-Islanders all she had got?"

"Edna also. But when she looked in, eleven days after Carol, she did not have the same scope for self-expression. Carol had caught us unprepared, but we were ready for Edna. Baths had been filled with water, candles laid in. Conditions under Carol would have brought a startled 'Gee whiz!' to the lips of King Lear, but Edna was a flop. A dramatic critic who was staying in Nantucket at the time of her arrival gave her a bad notice, being rather severe about her lack of significant form and uncertain direction of interest. Apparently, when she got to Nantucket, she split in two."

"One of those road shows that turn into turkeys."

"You said it."

"A thing about hurricanes that puzzles me is why Cape Hatteras affects them so emotionally."

"I know what you mean. Everything is fine up to there—wind at five miles an hour, practically a dead calm—but the moment a hurricane sees Cape Hatteras it quivers in every limb and starts blowing 125 m.p.h."

"Hysteria?"

"Possibly. But why?"

"It's odd, is it not? And here is another odd thing. Everything in America that you have criticized turns out to have its bright side."

"Not pigeons."

"No, not pigeons, but everything else. The income tax

gives solidarity to the American home. The mosquito provides unforgettable days on shikar. And the hurricane proves to be a blessing in disguise."

"I don't follow you there."

"I read in the paper that Carol put two hundred and sixty thousand telephones out of action. Surely this was an excellent thing. Is it not a pleasant thought that for three days Vera (aged sixteen) was not able to call up Clarice (fifteen and a half) and tell her what Jane had said about Alice? The father of many a family of growing girls, reveling in the unaccustomed peace, must have wondered why people made such a fuss about hurricanes. And, of course, during those three days there was no television."

"A-a-a-a-a-a-ah! Now you're talking!"

Gaughan the Deliverer

1

I SOMETIMES THINK I could endure television with more fortitude if they didn't laugh so much all the time.

Turning on the television set after reading the morning papers is like coming out of the shadows into a world of sunshine.

American papers today go in exclusively for gloom. I never saw so many people viewing with concern and contemplating with the gravest apprehension as are writing now for the daily press of the country. Talk about looking on the dark side. The only ones who do not prophesy the collapse of civilization at 3:30 sharp (Eastern Standard Time) a week from Wednesday are those who make it Tuesday afternoon at 2:45. But twiddle that knob and everything is joy and happiness and the laughter of little children.

At least, one assumes that they are little children. On the evidence submitted I would say their mental age was about six. Everybody is laughing on television these days. The studio audiences have, of course, been laughing themselves sick for years on the most flimsy provocation, but now the contagion has spread to the performers.

The other day John Crosby—not to be confused with Bing, Bing sings—John is the fellow who watches television for the New York *Herald Tribune,* than which I can imagine no more appalling job—just think of *having* to watch television—you don't catch John Crosby singing—he groans a good deal probably, so that you may think he is singing, but . . . Where was I? I seem to have lost the thread. Ah, yes, John Crosby. My reason for bringing him up was that he was complaining the other day about the time when Senator Margaret Chase Smith interviewed the Burmese Premier U Nu, on television and U Nu was so doubled up with laughter throughout that you could scarcely follow what he was saying. It came out something like this:

"If aggression—ha, ha, ha—comes from a foe—ha, ha, ha—the United Nations are quite ready to pass resolutions condemning that foe, but—wait, folks, you ain't heard nothin' yet—when aggression comes from friends, they like—this is going to slay you—they like to keep a little quiet—ha, ha, ha—or even if they are not quiet, they don't do full justice, ho, ho, ho."

The whole punctuated with roars of merriment from the

studio audience. No wonder John Crosby screams thinly and jumps six feet straight up in the air if you tap him unexpectedly on the shoulder. Just a bundle of nerves, our John.

The gruesome thing, to my mind—and mine is not a mind to be sneezed at—is that this is not always the laughter of a real studio audience. Frequently, it is canned or bottled. They preserve it on sound tracks, often dating back for years, so that what you are getting is the mummified mirth of people who, in many cases, died way back in about 1946, and if that is not an eerie thought, what is? "The voice I hear this passing night was heard In ancient days by emperor and clown," as Keats put it, switching off the comedy program.

Furthermore, somebody has invented what is known as a laugh machine which can produce completely artificial laughter. The man in charge of it keeps pressing a button at intervals during the cross-talk act, and the comedians love it.

Living-laughter studio audiences, as opposed to laugh machines and those indomitable wraiths who, in spite of having passed beyond the veil, are still in the highest spirits and always ready to do their bit, seem to be governed by some code of rules, probably unwritten and conveyed by word of mouth, for it is surely straining the probabilities a good deal to assume that a studio audience can read. It is a code subject to alteration without notice, and a certain amount of confusion sometimes results. Thus, it used to be obligatory to laugh whenever anyone on the television screen mentioned Brooklyn. If there was one credo rooted in the minds of the citizenry it was that the word Brooklyn was cachinnogenic. And now there has been a shift in the party line, and today you have to laugh at Texas.

Nobody knows why. It is just an order that has come down from the men higher up. It is perfectly permissible under the new rules to keep a straight face when somebody speaks of Oshkosh, Kalamazoo or the Gowanus Canal, but a studio audience which fails to laugh at the story of the Texan who refused steak *aux champignons* because he did not like champagne poured over his steak soon finds itself purged. The secret police are knocking at its door before it knows where it is.

But there is a fine spirit stirring in America these days, I am glad to say, as fine as that of '76. The people are on the march. The other day someone whipped out a revolver and shot his television set, and a week or so ago there was a still more impressive demonstration. Folks, let me lead by the hand into the Hall of Fame, Richard Gaughan.

At one-thirty in the afternoon of what will no doubt be known as Gaughan's Day and celebrated as a national festival, Richard Gaughan (29), of 75 Sherman Avenue, entered the studio of the Columbia Broadcasting Company during the rehearsal of a television show, armed with an eight-inch carving knife.

"I hate all television!" he announced. "I hate commentators. I hate the whole lousy bunch. There ought to be a law against television. I want to kill a TV operator."

Having spoken these words, which must have touched a responsive chord in many a bosom, this splendid fellow proceeded to stab a cameraman and to hit the producer on the frontal bone with a carafe. And lest you purse your lips at the latter statement, saying to yourselves "Hullo! What's this? Did Gaughan weaken?" I must explain that a carafe, picked up on the set, was all he had to work with. After he stabbed the cameraman, the knife broke. He had paid only fifty-nine cents for it, not reflecting that you cannot get a really good carving knife as cheap as that. If you are going to stab cameramen, it is always wisest to go as high as a dollar.

It was as he was about to attack the director that the police came in and scooped him up, a sad disappointment to the better element. It appears that there is some law against wiping out television directors with carafes, one of those strange laws that get passed occasionally, nobody knows why.

Where Richard Gaughan—Gaughan the Deliverer most of us are calling him now—went wrong, in my opinion, was in confining his activities to a rehearsal, for by doing so he missed the studio audience. He should have bided his time till one of these gangs had been assembled.

Where everything about television is so frightful, it is difficult to say which is its most repulsive feature, but the majority of connoisseurs would, I think, pick the studio audience. If it would only stay quiet, nobody would have any complaint, but it won't. It laughs like a congregation of hyenas at everything. The other night on what was for some reason described as a comedy program a girl said to a man, "You are selfish."

To which he replied: "How dare you call me a shellfish?"

The studio audience let out a bellow of mirth which was audible as far downtown as the Battery, and all over America strong men gritted their teeth and muttered, "Gaughan, thou shouldst be living at this hour!"

But a time will come. In ninety days or whatever it is he will be with us once more. Good hunting, Richard Gaughan. And don't make that mistake again of trying to do it on the cheap. Avoid bargain prices. Even if it costs as much as two dollars, get a good knife.

2

From the foregoing remarks you may have formed the impression that I dislike television. I would not go so far as to say that. Apart from thinking it the foulest, ghastliest, loathsomest nightmare ever inflicted by science on a suffering human race and the programs, except for the Wednesday and Friday night fights, the most driveling half-witted productions ever seen outside Guest Night at a home for the feeble-minded, I do not particularly object to it. As far as I am concerned, it can carry on, provided—I say provided —I have not to excite the derision of the mob by appearing on the screen myself.

But how often this happens. Every time I have a new book out, it comes again . . . the Finger. The telephone rings, and it is my publishers' publicity man informing me briskly that I am to appear on television next week—Monday 8:30, Sonny Booch's Strictly for Morons half-hour; Tuesday, 9:15, Alonzo Todd's Park Your Brains in the

Cloakroom; and Thursday, 7:35, Genevieve Goole Pobsleigh's Life Among the Halfwits.

You might suppose from all this that there is a great popular demand for me, that America wants Wodehouse and refuses to be put off with President Eisenhower, Mary Martin and similar cheap substitutes, but this is not so. There may be men in the United States more insignificant than myself, men whose names mean even less to the far-flung citizenry, but they would take a bit of finding. Bloodhounds would be needed and Private Eyes with magnifying glasses. No, the explanation is that this publicity man thinks it will boost the sales of my book if I am seen by millions on the television screen, not realizing, poor deluded soul, that the one way of slaying a book is to let the people get a look at the author.

Authors as a class are no oil paintings. You have only to go to one of those literary dinners to test the truth of this. At such a binge you will see tall authors, short authors, stout authors, thin authors and authors of medium height and girth, but all of these authors without exception look like something that would be passed over with a disdainful jerk of the beak by the least fastidious buzzard in the Gobi desert. Only very rarely do we find one who has even the most rudimentary resemblance to anything part-human.

If they wanted to interview me on the radio, that would be different. I might do myself a bit of good by saying a few graceful words on the radio. I have an attractive voice, rich, mellow, with certain deep organ tones in it calculated to make quite a number of the cash customers dig up the $3.50. But it is fatal to let them see me.

Owing to my having become mentally arrested at an early age, I write the sort of books which people, not knowing the facts, assume to be the work of a cheerful, if backward, young fellow of about twenty-five. "Well, well," they tell one another, "we might do worse than hear what this youngster has to say. Get the rising generation point of view, and all that." And what happens? "We have with us tonight, Mr. P. G. Wodehouse" . . . and on totters a spavined septuagenarian, his bald head coated with pancake flour to keep it from shining and his palsied limbs twitching feebly like those of a galvanized frog. Little wonder that when the half-yearly score sheet reaches me some months later I find that sales have been what publishers call "slow" again. America's book-buyers have decided as one book-buyer to keep the money in the old oak chest, and I don't blame them. I wouldn't risk a nickel on anyone who looks as I do on the television screen.

I have never understood this theory that you don't get the full flavor of a writer's work unless you see him. On every newspaper staff in America there are half a dozen columnists, and every day each of these columnists has his photograph at the head of his column. All wrong it seems to me. I mean, after you have seen Westbrook Pegler or Hy Gardner three or four hundred days in succession you have had practically all you require and their spell wanes. It is a significant thing, I think, that the greatest of all columnists, Walter Winchell, who has led the field for a matter of twenty-five years, has never allowed his photograph to appear. And Walter is a good-looking man, too, not unlike what I was in my prime.

That is the maddening thing about this television business, that they are catching me too late. "Oh, God, put back Thy universe and give me yesterday," as the fellow said. Well, no, not yesterday perhaps, but say 1906 or thereabouts. I really was an eyeful then. Trim athletic figure, finely chiseled features and more hair on the top of my head than you could shake a stick at. I would have been more than willing to exhibit myself to America's millions then. But now I have definitely gone off quite a bit, and that is why, when this publicity man calls up and starts persecuting me with his loathsome addresses, I have my answer ready, quick as a flash.

"Terribly sorry," I say. "I'm just off to the Coast."

Heaven bless the Coast. It is the one safe refuge. Even press representatives or public relations lizards or whatever they call themselves know they can't get at you there. And these constant visits to the Coast are improving my prestige. "Wodehouse always seems to be going to Hollywood," people say. "Yes," reply the people these people are addressing, "the demand for him in the studios is tremendous." "Odd one never sees his name on screen credits," say the first people. "Oh, no." (Second people speaking.) "He writes under a number of pseudonyms. Makes a fortune, I understand."

The Girl in the Pink Bathing Suit

1

As a matter of fact, I have been to Hollywood, though not recently. I went there in 1930. I had a year's contract, and was required to do so little work in return for the money I received that I was able in the twelve months before I became a fugitive from the chain gang to write a novel and fourteen short stories, besides brushing up my golf, getting an attractive suntan and perfecting my Australian crawl in the swimming pool.

It is all sadly changed now, they tell me. Once a combination of Santa Claus and Good-Time Charlie, Hollywood has become a Scrooge. The dear old days are dead and the spirit of cheerful giving a thing of the past. But in 1930 the talkies had just started, and the slogan was Come one, come all, and the more the merrier. It was an era when only a man of exceptional ability and determination could keep from getting signed up by a studio in some capacity or other. I happened to be engaged as a writer, but I might quite as easily have been scooped in as a technical adviser or a vocal instructor. (At least I had a roof to my mouth, which many vocal instructors in Hollywood at that time had not.) The heartiness and hospitality reminded one of the Jolly Innkeeper (with entrance number in Act One) of the old-style comic opera.

One can understand it, of course. The advent of sound had made the manufacture of motion pictures an infinitely more complex affair than it had been up till then. In the silent days everything had been informal and casual, just a lot of great big happy schoolboys getting together for a bit of fun. Ike would have a strip of celluloid, Spike a camera his uncle had given him for Christmas, Mike would know a friend or two who liked dressing up and having their photographs taken, and with these modest assets they would club together their pocket money and start the Finer and Supremer Films Corporation. And as for bothering about getting anyone to write them a story, it never occurred to them. They made it up themselves as they went along.

The talkies changed all that. It was no longer possible

just to put on a toga, have someone press a button and call the result *The Grandeur that Was Rome* or *In the Days of Nero.* A whole elaborate new organization was required. You had to have a studio Boss to boss the Producer, a Producer to produce the Supervisor, a Supervisor to supervise the sub-Supervisor, a sub-Supervisor to sub-supervise the Director, a Director to direct the Camera Man and an Assistant Director to assist the Director. And, above all, you had to get hold of someone to supply the words.

The result was a terrible shortage of authors in all the world's literary centers. New York till then had been full of them. You would see them frisking in perfect masses in any editorial office you happened to enter. Their sharp, excited yapping was one of the features of the first or second act intermission of every new play that was produced. And in places like Greenwich Village you had to watch your step very carefully to avoid treading on them.

And then all of a sudden all you saw was an occasional isolated one being shooed out of a publisher's sanctum or sitting in a speakeasy sniffing at his press clippings. Time after time fanciers would come up to you with hard-luck stories.

"You know that novelist of mine with the flapping ears and the spots on his coat? Well, he's gone."

"Gone?"

"Absolutely vanished. I left him on the steps of the club, and when I came out there were no signs of him."

"Same here," says another fancier. "I had a brace of

playwrights to whom I was greatly attached, and they've disappeared without a word."

Well, of course, people took it for granted that the little fellows had strayed and had got run over, for authors are notoriously dreamy in traffic and, however carefully you train them, will persist in stopping in the middle of the street to jot down strong bits of dialogue. It was only gradually that the truth came out. They had all been decoyed away to Hollywood.

What generally happened was this. A couple of the big film executives—say Mr. Louis B. Mayer and Mr. Adolf Zukor—would sight their quarry in the street and track him down to some bohemian eating resort. Having watched him settle, they seat themselves at a table immediately behind him, and for a few moments there is silence, broken only by the sound of the author eating corned beef hash. Then Mr. Mayer addresses Mr. Zukor, raising his voice slightly.

"Whatever was the name of that girl?" he says.

"What girl?" asks Mr. Zukor, cleverly taking his cue.

"That tall, blonde girl with the large blue eyes."

"The one in the pink bathing suit?"

"That's right. With the freckle in the small of her back."

"A freckle? A mole, I always understood."

"No, it was a freckle, eyewitnesses tell me. Just over the base of the spinal cord. Well, anyway, what was her name?"

"Now what was it? Eulalie something? Clarice something? No, it's gone. But I'll find out for you when we get home. I know her intimately."

Here they pause, but not for long. There is a sound of quick, emotional breathing. The author is standing beside them, a rapt expression on his face.

"Pardon me, gentlemen," he says, "for interrupting a private conversation, but I chanced to overhear you saying that you were intimately acquainted with a tall, blonde girl with large blue eyes, in the habit of wearing bathing suits of just the type I like best. It is for a girl of that description that I have been scouring the country for years. Where may she be found?"

"In God's Back Garden—Hollywood," says Mr. Zukor.

"Pity you can't meet her," says Mr. Mayer. "You're just her type."

"If you were by any chance an author," says Mr. Zukor, "we could take you back with us tomorrow. Too bad you're not."

"Prepare yourselves for a surprise, gentlemen," says the victim. "I *am* an author. George Montague Breamworthy. 'Powerfully devised situations'—New York *Times*. 'Sheer, stark realism'—New York *Herald Tribune*. 'Whoops!'—*Women's Wear*.' "

"In that case," says Mr. Mayer, producing a contract, "sign here."

"Where my thumb is," says Mr. Zukor.

The trap has snapped.

2

That was how they got me, and it was, I understand, the usual method of approach. But sometimes this plan failed, and then sterner methods were employed. The demand for authors in those early talkie days was so great that it led to the revival of the old press-gang. Nobody was safe even if he merely looked like an author.

While having a Malted Milk Greta Garbo with some of the old lags in the commissary one morning about halfway through my term of sentence, I was told of one very interesting case. It appeared that there was a man who had gone out West hoping to locate oil. One of those men without a thought in the world outside of oil; the last thing he had ever dreamed of doing was being an author. With the exception of letters and an occasional telegram of greeting to some relative at Christmas, he had never written anything in his life.

But, by some curious chance, it happened that his appearance was that of one capable of the highest feats in the way of literary expression. He had a domelike head, piercing eyes, and that cynical twist of the upper lip which generally means an epigram on the way. Still, as I say, he was not a writer, and no one could have been more surprised than he was when, walking along a deserted street in Los Angeles, thinking of oil, he was suddenly set upon by masked men, chloroformed, and whisked away in a closed car. When he came to himself he was in a cell on the Perfecto-Zizzbaum lot with paper and a sharpened pencil before him, and stern-featured men in felt hats and raincoats were waggling rubber hoses at him and telling him to get busy and turn out something with lots of sex in it, but not too much, because of Will Hays.

The story has a curious sequel. A philosopher at heart, he accepted the situation. He wrenched his mind away from oil and scribbled a few sentences that happened to occur to him. He found, as so many have found, that an author's is the easiest job in existence, and soon he was scratching away as briskly as you could wish. And that is how Noel Coward got his start.

But not every kidnaped author accepted his fate so equably. The majority endeavored to escape. But it was useless. Even if the rigors of the pitiless California climate did not drive them back to shelter, capture was inevitable. When I was in Hollywood there was much indignation among the better element of the community over the pursuit of an unfortunate woman writer whom the harshness of her supervisor, a man of the name of Legree, had driven to desperation. As I got the story, they chased her across the ice with bloodhounds.

The whole affair was very unpleasant and shocked the softhearted greatly. So much so that a Mrs. Harriet Beecher Stowe told me that if M.G.M. would meet her terms for the movie, she intended to write a book about it which would stir the world.

"Boy," she said to me, "it will be a scorcher!"
I don't know if anything ever came of it.

3

I got away from Hollywood at the end of the year because the jailer's daughter smuggled me in a file in a meat pie, but I was there long enough to realize what a terribly demoralizing place it is. The whole atmosphere there is one of insidious deceit and subterfuge. Nothing is what it affects to be. What looks like a tree is really a slab of wood backed with barrels. What appears on the screen as the towering palace of Haroun-al-Raschid is actually a cardboard model occupying four feet by three of space. The languorous lagoon is simply a smelly tank with a stagehand named Ed wading about in it in bathing trunks.

It is surely not difficult to imagine the effect of all this on a sensitive-minded author. Taught at his mother's knee to love the truth, he finds himself surrounded by people making fortunes by what can only be called chicanery. After a month or two in such an environment could you trust that author to count his golf shots correctly or to give his right sales figures?

And then there was—I am speaking of the old days. It is possible that modern enlightened thought has brought improvements—the inevitable sapping of his self-respect. At the time of which I am writing authors in Hollywood were kept in little hutches. In every studio there were rows and rows of these, each containing an author on a long contract at a weekly salary. You could see their anxious little faces peering out through the bars and hear them whining piteously to be taken for a walk. One had to be very callous not to be touched by such a spectacle.

I do not say that these authors were actually badly treated. In the best studios in those early talkie days kindness was the rule. Often you would see some high executive stop and give one of them a lettuce. And it was the same with the humaner type of director. In fact, between the directors and their authors there frequently existed a rather touching friendship. I remember one director telling a story which illustrates this.

One morning, he said, he was on his way to his office, preoccupied, as was his habit when planning out the day's work, when he felt a sudden tug at his coattails. He looked down and there was his pet author, Edgar Montrose (Book Society Recommendation) Delamere. The little fellow had got him in a firm grip and was gazing up at him, in his eyes an almost human expression of warning.

Well, the director, not unnaturally, mistook this at first for mere playfulness, for it was often his kindly habit to romp with his little charges. Then something seemed to whisper to him that he was being withheld from some great peril. He remembered stories he had read as a boy—one of which he was even then directing for Rin-Tin-Tin—where faithful dogs dragged their masters back from the brink of precipices on dark nights, and, scarcely knowing why, he turned and went off to the commissary and had a Strawbery and Vanilla Nut Sundae Mary Pickford.

It was well that he did. In his office, waiting to spring, there was lurking a foreign star with a bad case of temperament, whose bite might have been fatal. You may be sure that Edgar Montrose had a good meal that night.

But that was an isolated case. Not all directors were like this one. Too many of them crushed the spirit of the captives by incessant blue-penciling of their dialogue, causing them to become listless and lose appetite. Destructive criticism is what kills an author. Cut his material too much, make him feel that he is not a Voice, give him the impression that his big scene is all wet, and you will soon see the sparkle die out of his eyes.

I don't know how conditions are today, but at that time there were authors who had been on salary for years in Hollywood without ever having a line of their work used. All they did was attend story conferences. There were other authors whom nobody had seen for years. It was like the Bastille. They just sat in some hutch away in a corner somewhere and grew white beards and languished. From time to time somebody would renew their contract, and then they were forgotten again.

As I say, it may be different now. After all, I am speaking of twenty-five years ago. But I do think it would be wise if author-fanciers exercised vigilance. You never know. The press-gang may still be in our midst.

So when you take your pet for a walk, keep an eye on him. If he goes sniffing after strange men, whistle him back.

And remember that the spring is the dangerous time. Around about the beginning of May, authors get restless and start dreaming about girls in abbreviated swim suits. It is easy to detect the symptoms. The moment you hear yours muttering about the Golden West and God's Sunshine and Out There Beyond the Stifling City put sulphur in his absinthe and lock him up in the kitchenette.

Francis Bacon and the Play Doctor

1

AND NOW Ho for a chapter on the theater and what I have done to put it on the map.

A dramatist friend of mine was telling me the other day that he had written his last play. He was embittered because the star for whom he had been waiting for two years backed out on obtaining a big television contract and another star for whom he had been waiting two years before that suddenly went off to Hollywood. And this after he had worked like a beaver rewriting his play to suit the views of the manager, the manager's wife, the principal backer and the principal backer's son, a boy of some fourteen summers named

Harold, on whose judgment the principal backer placed great reliance.

Furthermore, he said, he could no longer face those out-of-town preliminary tours, with their "Nobody comes to the theater on Monday in these small towns. Wait till Tuesday," "Well, Tuesday, everyone knows, is a bad night everywhere. Wait till Wednesday," and "You can't get 'em into the theater on a Wednesday. Wait till Thursday. Thursday will tell the story." And always the manager at his elbow, chewing two inches of an unlighted cigar and muttering, "Well, boy, there ain't no doubt but what it's going to need a lot of work."

Myself, I have never regretted my flirtations with the drama. They cost me a lot of blood, sweat and tears, not to mention making me lose so much hair that nowadays I am often mistaken in a dim light for a Hallowe'en pumpkin, but one met such interesting people. I have encountered in the coulisses enough unforgettable characters to fix up the *Reader's Digest* for years and years. Most of these are enshrined in the pages of a book called *Bring on the Girls* which Guy Bolton and I wrote not long ago.

My first play was written in collaboration with a boy named Henry Cullimore when I was pushing seven. I don't quite know what made us decide to do it, but we did so decide, and Henry said we would have to have a plot. "What's a plot?" I asked. He didn't know. He had read or heard somewhere that a plot was a good thing to have, but as to what it was he confessed himself fogged. This naturally made us both feel a little stymied, but we agreed that there was nothing to do but carry on and hope that everything would pan out all right. (Chekhov used to do this.)

He—Henry Cullimore, not Chekhov—was the senior partner in the project. He was two or three years older than I was, which gave him an edge, and he had a fountain pen. I mostly contributed moral support, pursuing the same method which I later found to answer so well when I teamed up with Guy Bolton. When Guy and I pitched in on a play, he would do the rough spadework—the writing —and I used to look in on him from time to time and say "How are you getting on?" He would say, "All right," and I would say, "Fine," and go off and read Agatha Christie. Giving it the Wodehouse Touch, I used to call it. And so little by little and bit by bit the thing would get done.

This system worked capitally with all the Bolton-Wodehouse productions, and I believe it was the way Beaumont and Fletcher used to hammer out their combined efforts. ("How goeth it, my heart of gold?" "Yarely, old mole. Well, fairly yarely." "Stick at it, boy. Hard work never hurt anyone.") But Henry Cullimore let me down. A broken reed, if ever there was one. He got as far as

---

ACT ONE

(*Enter Henry*)

HENRY: What's for breakfast? Ham and oatmeal? Very nice.

but there he stopped. He had shot his bolt.

How he was planning to go on if the divine afflatus had not blown a fuse, I never discovered. I should imagine that the oatmeal proved to be poisoned—("One of the barbiturate group, Inspector, unless I am greatly mistaken") —or a dead body dropped out of the closet where they kept the sugar.

The thing was never produced. A pity, for I think it would have been a great audience show.

Since then I have been mixed up in sixteen straight plays and twenty-two musical comedies as author, part author or just hanging on to the author in the capacity of Charles his friend. In virtually every theatrical enterprise there is a Charles his friend, drawing his weekly royalties. Nobody ever quite knows how he wriggled in, but there he is. Affability of manner has a good deal to do with it.

But though I attached myself to these straight plays, some of them the most outstanding flops in the history of the stage, my heart was never really in them. Musical comedy was my dish, the musical comedy theater my spiritual home. I would rather have written *Oklahoma!* than *Hamlet*. (Actually, as the records show, I wrote neither, but you get the idea.)

It was in 1904 that I burst on the theatrical scene with a lyric in a thing called *Sergeant Brue* at the Prince of Wales Theater in London. In 1906 I got a job at two pounds a week as a sort of utility lyricist at the Aldwych Theater in the same town. This, as I have already recorded, involved writing some numbers with a young American composer named Jerome Kern, and when, a good many years later, I ran into him and Guy Bolton in New York, we got together and did what were known as the Princess shows, hot stuff in their day. After that I worked with Victor Herbert, George Gershwin, Rudolf Friml, Vincent Youmans, Emmerich Kalman, Ivan Caryll, Franz Lehar and what seems to me now about a hundred other composers. For years scarcely a day passed whose low descending sun did not see me at my desk trying to find some rhyme for "June" that would not be "soon," "moon," "tune" or "spoon." (Billy Rose at the outset of his career suddenly thought of "macaroon" and from that moment never looked back.)

It is not to be wondered at, then, that when I can spare a moment of my valuable time, I find myself brooding on the musical comedy theater of today. The subject is one of compelling interest. What is going to happen to it? Can it last? If so, how much longer? Will there come a day when we reach out for it and find it isn't there? Are the rising costs of production ever going to stop rising? And if they don't stop rising, what will the harvest be? It is difficult enough to prize the required two hundred and fifty thousand dollars out of the investing public now. What of tomorrow, when it will probably be half a million?

Have you ever tried to touch anyone for two hundred

and fifty thousand dollars? It is by no means the same thing as asking for a five till Wednesday, old man. It takes doing. Howard Dietz, on whom be peace, once wrote an opening chorus for a revue which Max Gordon produced. It ran:

> What's all that cheering in the streets?
> What's all that cheering you're
> hearing in the streets?
> Max Gordon's raised the money,
> Max Gordon's raised the money . . .

and while joining in the cheering, one cannot help dropping a silent tear as one thinks of what Max must have gone through. And in his capacity of prominent Broadway manager, he presumably had to do it again and again and again.

How anyone who has once raised the money for a New York musical can bring himself to do it a second time, is more than I can imagine. A few years ago a management decided that the moment had come to revive a show with which I had been connected somewhere around 1920 and asked me to come to a "backers' audition." I was there through the grim proceedings, and came away feeling like one of those can-you-spare-a-nickel-for-a-cup-of-coffee gentlemen of leisure who pop up through the sidewalk in front of you as you take your walks abroad down Washington Square way. My hat, quite a good one, seemed battered and shapeless, there were cracks in the uppers of my shoes, and an unwholesome growth of hair had sprouted on my cheeks, accompanied by a redness and swelling of the nose. I felt soiled. (There were headlines in all the papers—WODEHOUSE FEELS SOILED.)

A backers' audition is composed of cringing mendicants —the management, a pianist, some hired singers and some friends and supporters who are there to laugh and applaud —and a little group of fat, rich men with tight lips and faces carved out of granite, whom you have assembled somehow and herded into a hotel suite. These are the backers, or it might be better to say you hope they are the backers, for while there is unquestionably gold in them thar heels, the problem is how to extract it.

Cigars, drinks and caviar have been provided, and the management proceeds to read the script, pausing at intervals to allow the hired singers to render the songs. The fat, rich men sit there with their eyes bulging, in a silence broken only by the champing of jaws and a musical gurgle as another highball goes down the gullet, and then, loaded to the Plimsoll mark with caviar, they file out, not having uttered a word.

And this goes on and on. In order to collect the money to produce *Oklahoma!* eighty-nine of these auditions had to be given. I imagine that it was not till about the sixty-third that somebody stirred in his chair and brought out a checkbook. Perhaps one of the songs had touched his heart, reminding him of something his mother used to sing when he clustered about her knee, or possibly conscience whispered to him that as he was all that caviar ahead of the game, he ought to do something about it. So he wrote his check.

But for how much? Ten thousand? Twenty thousand? Even if it was fifty thousand it merely scratched the surface. It is a matter of record that *Oklahoma!* was still twenty thousand short when it opened out of town, and would never have been brought into New York if S. N. Behrman had not come to the rescue.

However, let us suppose that somehow you have contrived to wheedle two hundred and fifty thousand dollars out of the money classes. What then? You are then faced with the prospect of having to play to thirty-three thousand a week simply to break even. I was shown the weekly balance sheet of an apparently very prosperous musical comedy the other day. The gross box-office receipts were $36,442.90, which sounds fine, but after all expenses had been paid the profit on the week was $3,697.83. I am no mathematician, but it looked to me as if they would have to go on doing about $37,000 a week for about a year and a half before the backers drew a cent. No wonder these prudent men are often inclined to settle for free cigars and caviar and not get mixed up in all that sordid business of paying out money.

That is why if you ever catch me in pensive mood, sitting with the chin supported in the hand and the elbow on the knee, like Rodin's "Thinker," you can be pretty sure that I am saying to myself, "Whither the New York musical comedy theater?" or possibly, "The New York musical comedy theater . . . whither?" It is a question that constantly exercises me. I can't see what, as the years roll by and costs continue to rise, is going to happen to the bally thing.

Financing a straight play is, of course, simpler, but even this is not easy. Perhaps the best plan is to follow the example of a recent manager who induced a rich acquaintance to part with the necessary cash by reading him Eugene O'Neill's *The Hairy Ape*.

"Good, don't you think?" he said.

"Terrific," said the rich acquaintance. The manager then used the money to put on a bedroom farce which he had written, and when the backer saw it on the opening night in Philadelphia, he was a little puzzled.

"But this isn't the play you read me," he said.

"Oh, well," said the manager, "you know how these things always get changed around a bit at rehearsals."

2

It is the stagehand situation that causes a good deal of the present unrest. This situation—I am speaking of the stagehand situation—is quite a situation. The trouble—briefly—is this. Stagehands cost money, and theatrical managers hate parting with money. The scene-shifter's union, on the other hand, is all for it. Blow the expense, says the scene-shifter's union. It likes to see money scattered in handfuls, always provided it is someone else's (or someone's else, as the case may be). This leads to strained relations, pique on both sides and the calling of some most unpleasant names. I have heard managers refer to the union as vampires, while the union, speaking of the managers, is far too prone to make nasty cracks about people who are so tight they could carry an armful of eels up six flights of stairs and never drop one of them.

Most plays nowadays are in one set, and a manager who puts on a one-set play feels that once this one set is in position he ought to be able to pay the scene-shifters off and kiss them good-by. He sees no reason why he should have to pay a weekly wage to a gang of scene-shifters just for not shifting scenes. All he wants is an operative who will go over the set from time to time with a feather duster, to keep the moths from getting into it.

The union does not take this view. It holds that if the manager hasn't any scenes to shift he darned well ought to have, and it insists on him employing the number of scene-shifters who would have been required to shift the scenes if there had been any scenes to shift, if you follow me. And as any attempt to brook the will of the union leads to a strike of stagehands, which leads to a strike of electricians, which leads to a strike of actors, box-office officials, gentlemanly ushers and the theater cat, it gets its way. Thus we find Ruth Draper, who does her stuff with no scenery at all, obliged during her latest engagement to employ seven stagehands. Victor Borge, giving a two-hour solo performance on the piano at the Booth, had eight. (Why this discrimination?) And a recent one-set comedy with three characters in it was attended nightly by no fewer than fifteen admirers and well-wishers. Some plays these last seasons have suffered from audience thinness, but no manager has ever run short of stagehands. They are there from the moment the curtain goes up, with their hair in a braid.

At the risk of becoming too technical, I must explain briefly how a troupe of stagehands with nothing to do is organized. There is, I need scarcely say, nothing haphazard about it. First-chosen by show of hands (stagehands)—comes the head man or Giant Sloth. His job is to hang upside down from a rafter. Next we have the Senior Lounger and the Junior Lounger, who lie on couches—Roman fashion—with chaplets of roses around their foreheads. Last comes the rank and file, the twelve Lilies of the Field. It was because I was uncertain as to the duties of these that I looked in the other night at one of the theaters to get myself straight on the point, and was courteously received by the Junior Lounger, a Mr. B. J. Wilberforce, who showed no annoyance at being interrupted while working on his crossword puzzle.

"I was wondering, Mr. Wilberforce," I said, when greetings and compliments had been exchanged, "if you could tell me something about this situation."

"What situation would that be?" he asked.

"The scene-shifter situation," I said, and he frowned.

"We prefer not to be called scene-shifters," he explained. "There seems to us something a little vulgar about shifting scenes. It smacks too much of those elaborate musical productions, where, I am told, the boys often get quite hot and dusty. We of the elite like to think of ourselves as America's leisure class. Of course, when there is work to be done, we do it. Only the other night, for instance, the director thought that it would brighten things up if an upstage chair were moved to a downstage position. We were called into conference, and long before the curtain rose for the evening's performance the thing was done. Superintended by the Giant Sloth, we Loungers—myself and my immediate superior, Cyril Muspratt—each grasped one side of the seat and that chair was moved, and it would have been the same if it had been two chairs. I am not saying it did not take it out of us. It did. But we do not spare ourselves when the call comes."

"Still, it does not come often, I suppose? As a general rule, you have your leisure?"

"Oh, yes. We have lots of time to fool around in."

"Never end a sentence with a preposition, Wilberforce," I said warningly, and he blushed. I had spoken kindly, but you could see it stung.

At this moment somebody on the stage said in a loud voice: "My God! My wife!"—they were playing one of those Victorian farce revivals designed to catch the nostalgia trade—and he winced.

"All this noise!" he said. "One realizes that actors have to make a living, but there is no need for a lot of racket and disturbance. It is most disagreeable for a man doing his crossword puzzle and trying to concentrate on a word in three letters beginning with E and signifying 'large Australian bird' to be distracted by sudden sharp cries. Still, it might be worse. At the Bijou, where they are doing one of those gangster things, the Giant Sloth was often woken three or four times in an evening by pistol shots. He had to complain about it, and now, I believe, the actors just say, 'Bang, bang!' in an undertone. Three letters beginning with E," he mused.

I knew it could not be the Sun God Ra. Then suddenly I got it.

"Emu!"

"I beg your pardon?"

"That large Australian bird you were speaking of."

"Of which you were speaking. Never end a sentence with a preposition, Wodehouse."

Sensing that tempers were rising, I bade him good night and went on my way. So I still don't know how those Lilies of the Field fill in their time. Perhaps they just catch up with their reading.

They tell a tale in Shubert Alley of a manager who walked one day on Forty-fifth Street west of Broadway and paused to watch workmen razing the Avon Theater.

"Gosh!" he said, much moved. "They're using fewer

men to tear down the building than we used to have to hire to strike a one-set show."

And there, gentle reader, let us leave him.

3

One enormous improvement in the theater of today is the almost total disappearance of the play doctor or play fixer or whatever he liked to call himself. The best description of this pest is the one given by George S. Kaufman in his 1925 comedy, *The Butter and Egg Man.* In Act Two, while the after-the-opening-at-Syracuse conference is in progress, there is a knock at the door, and Bernie Sampson comes in.

"Bernie Sampson," says Mr. Kaufman, "is a young man with that air of sophistication about him that can be acquired only through long service on Broadway. Once, many years before, he had made a suggestion for the improvement of a play that had just opened out of town. The suggestion was misunderstood by the producer, and the mistaken suggestion saved the play. Ever since then Bernie Sampson has been a recognized play fixer."

Shakespeare, the Baconians maintain, was nothing but a Bernie Sampson. All the work he did, they say, was to practice spelling his signature on the covers of the prompt copy, and in support of this contention a Baconian of my acquaintance tells a story which he claims is thoroughly documented—only unfortunately in a cipher which nobody but he can read.

It seems, according to this man, that Bacon, best known to the reading public of his day as the author of two bright little works entitled *Novum Organum* and *De Interpretatione Naturae,* had always had the firm conviction that he could write a play. He was, in short, a dreamer. (Aren't we all?) So in the intervals of looking after the Exchequer, of which, it will be remembered, he was the genial and popular Chancellor, he sat down with the old quill and inkhorn and dashed off a tragedy called *Hamlet.*

He then began sending it around to the managers.

The first manager kept it six months, and, when Bacon wrote enquiring after it, sent him back a farcical comedy by Marlowe, Ben Jonson and Peele, regretting that it was not in his power, much as he admired it personally, to produce the same.

Bacon sighed, and sent another copy to another manager.

When a year had elapsed, he wrote, apologizing for what might seem impatience on his part but asking if any decision on his drama *Hamlet* had been arrived at. Five weeks later, he received by the same post his manuscript and a letter from the manager saying that there had evidently been some mistake, for no such manuscript had come to his office.

By this time Bacon had begun to realize, as so many have realized since, that things theatrical are inseparable from a sort of brisk delirium usually associated only with the interiors of homes for those who have found the strain too much for them. And he had just decided to give the thing up and start on another book of essays when quite unexpectedly a manager who had had the script three years and had quite gone out of his mind (Bacon's mind), wrote asking him to call. And after waiting for four hours in the outer office with a crowd of blue-chinned men who were telling each other how they had jumped in and saved the show when they were with the Earl of Worcester's company, he was shown in.

"Now, this what's-it-name of yours," said the manager, "this *Hamlet*—of course, we'll have to change the title—I think it's got a chance. But it needs fixing. You're new to this game, I imagine?"

Bacon muttered something about having done a bit of writing.

"Plays?"

"Essays."

"Essays!" said the manager with a short laugh. "Well, as I was saying, we'll have to get the thing fixed. And the man to do it is young Shakespeare. Clever boy. In my company. He'll know what to do with it. Now about terms. You get one per cent of the gross."

Bacon, who as Chancellor of the Exchequer, was pretty good at figures, protested that one per cent of the gross was not enough.

"Now, sweetheart," said the manager—all right, I'll

come right out with it. It was Burbage—"Don't you begin opening your mouth too wide, like the rest of them. When you came into my office, I said to myself 'There's a sensible, level-headed young chap,' I said to myself. 'You won't find him wanting the earth.' You aren't going to make me alter my opinion? Of course you aren't. Why, if we do fifteen ducats, four pieces of eight and a rose noble on the Saturday night, you'll make a pile out of one per cent. Sign here."

A shrewd man, Bacon realized that there was nothing else for him to do. The superstition current in theatrical circles that there was a kind of magic in play-writing, and that nobody could fathom the mysteries of the craft unless he was one of the small coterie who spent their time in the Mermaid Tavern buying sack for managers, was too strong for him. He knew his *Hamlet* was good, but he had gathered by this time that he would never get it produced unless he consented to hand it over to the man who had been "twenty years in the business" to pull to pieces. So he signed the contract, and Burbage sent the office boy round to the Mermaid for Shakespeare.

A week later they all lunched together at that hostelry. Shakespeare had the script with him, and when the meal was over he took from his doublet a fat sheaf of notes.

"Well, kid," he said, "I've read that soap opera of yours. Of course there ain't no doubt but what it needs a lot of work. For one thing, your finish is weak. What you want at the final curtain is to have the whole crowd jump on one another and everybody kill everybody else. Lookut. The

King poisons the wine and Laertes poisons the sword and then Laertes plugs Hamlet with the sword and drops it and Hamlet picks it up in mistake for his own and plugs Laertes, and then the Queen drinks the poisoned wine and Hamlet sticks the King with the poisoned sword. Is that good, or is it good?"

"It's swell, Bill," said Burbage.

"But surely," said Bacon, "isn't all that a little improbable?"

"It's what the public wants," said Shakespeare coldly. "Or maybe you think I don't know?"

"Sure he knows you know, Bill," interposed Burbage soothingly. "Don't get your shirt out. We're all working for the good of the show. Is there anything else?"

"Is there anything else! Why, there's nothing else but something else. The whole thing's a mess."

"Is that so?" said Bacon.

"Yeah, this *is* so," said Shakespeare. "Why, you've made your hero a looney."

"His sufferings drove him mad," said Bacon.

"Not in any charade I'm going to have anything to do with his sufferings didn't," retorted Shakespeare. "Listen! I've been in this business twenty years——"

"And can't even spell your own name."

"I can too spell my own name."

"Well, what is it? Shakespeare, Shakspere, Shikspur or Shakspur? It comes out different every time."

"It does, does it?"

"Yes, it does."

"Well, be that as it may, you can't ask an audience to root for a looney."

Burbage intervened again.

" 'S all right, Bill," he said, patting Shakespeare's arm, " 's all right. Frankie knows that as well as we do. He gets the angle. You see, Frankie, we gotta think of the Wednesday matinee audiences. Wednesday matinee audiences don't like loonies. So you'll make him not crazy, Bill?"

"I'll do better than that. I'll make him *pretend* he's crazy. See? Everybody fooled but the audience."

"I told you this boy was clever," said Burbage to Bacon, who had turned rather pale and was beginning to pluck at the tablecloth.

"I still think he ought to be mad," he said.

"Well, I'll tell you what I'm sure Bill here will do to meet you, Frankie. He'll make the girl, Ophelia, mad. The customers don't mind a girl being crackers."

"All girls are crackers, anyway," said Shakespeare, speaking in rather a peevish tone, as if he had been reminded of some private grievances. He paused, and frowned thoughtfully as he turned his notes. " 'To be or not to be . . .' " he murmured, "I'm wondering about that 'To be or not to be' speech. They don't like soliloquies."

Bacon was now thoroughly aroused.

"Says you!"

"Yeah, says me."

"How about Elmer Rice and *Dream Girl*?"

"That's all right about Elmer Rice. Those Yanks'll do anything."

"Now, now, boys," said Burbage. "Hello, you leaving, Frankie?"

"Yes," said Bacon. "I am going to take a couple of aspirins and try to forget."

That is the story my Baconian acquaintance tells. And when I asked him how it came about that no mention of Bacon's share in the authorship has come down to us, he had his answer to that.

Shakespeare, he says, did offer to have the program read as follows:

HAMLET BY WILLIAM SHAKESPEARE

(Based on a suggestion by F. Bacon)

But Bacon, after sitting through a rehearsal or two and reading the revised script, decided to take his name off the bills.

Say It with Rattlesnakes

"AND NOW tell me, Mr. Wodehouse. You knew America when. What strikes you as the principal changes in the American scene—or, if you prefer it, the New York scene—since you first visited the country as a pie-faced lad in your early twenties fifty-one years ago? Come on, Grandpop. Last chapter. Say a few words."

"Well . . . New York scene, you said?"

"That's right."

"You don't want a lot of guff about Rockefeller Center and the Triborough Bridge?"

"No, no. Human interest stuff."

"Well, lemme think. Jussa minute. Changes? Principal changes?"

"Are there things, for instance, from the old days that you miss in these modern times?"

"Now you're talking. I miss those sacred concerts."

"Those—what was that once again?"

"Sacred concerts. On Sundays. When I first came to New York, they were the only form of Sunday entertainment the authorities would allow. They took place at the Palace or the Winter Garden, and began with some devotional exercises by Professor Wilkinson's Almost Human Seals, followed by the Hoopla Troupe, Acrobats Extraordinary, and Vokes and Dooley, the Somewhat Different Cross-Talk Comics. Then came Mick, Mac and Mabel in their Merry Mélange of Hoofing and Hilarity. Freddie Fitzgibbon, the Personality Kid, and so on through Vosper, the Ventriloquist and the Brothers Alonzo with their Jaunty Juggling to Sid Sterling and Company in the dramatic sketch 'She Was Only a Fireman's Daughter.' "

"Ah, yes, I see. Vaudeville shows."

"Nothing of the kind. Vaudeville shows, indeed! Do you think the City Fathers would have allowed vaudeville shows on Sunday? These were sacred concerts. The celebrants wore their ordinary clothes. That, in the view of the City Fathers, was the acid test. If you did your stuff in a green wig, purple dress clothes and a scarlet top hat, you were a vaudeville act. Stick to mufti, and you became a sacred concert. When Vokes enquired of Dooley the identity of the lady with whom he had seen him walking down the street, he was clad in blue serge. And when Dooley replied that his female companion was not a lady but his wife, he did it in a dotted herringbone suit with satin-lined sleeves and scallops on the pocket flaps. It was all very devout."

"No doubt you attribute your present depth of character to those sacred concerts?"

"A good deal of it. Call it two thirds."

"I'm sorry I was too young to join the congregation myself. It must have been most inspirational. An amusing little misunderstanding, that, between Vokes and Dooley."

"Oh, very."

"And what other changes have you noticed, Mr. Wodehouse?"

"Well, there's the American Christmas. It's not the simple festival it used to be. It seems to have got elephantiasis or something."

"We celebrate it, you mean, in a big way nowadays?"

"Too big, in my opinion. I don't want to do anyone an injustice, but the thought has sometimes crossed my mind that some of these department stores are trying to make money out of Christmas."

"Oh, surely not?"

"The idea horrifies you?"

"Intensely."

"It horrified Mr. Macy and Mr. Gimbel when I put it up to them. 'Absurd,' said Mr. Macy. 'Good heavens, no, dear old chap,' said Mr. Gimbel. But I still have my doubts. All these Santa Clauses pulling in the customers."

"Now there's a job I shouldn't care to have. Children crawling all over you."

"Yes, I was talking to one of them the other day in a drugstore where he had gone in his brief time off to refresh himself with a small wassail bowl. I asked him if he didn't ever falter. He gave me a look. He said that a Santa Claus who faltered would receive short shrift from his brother Santa Clauses. Before you could say 'Saks Fifth Avenue' he would find himself in a hollow square, being formally stripped of his whiskers and stomach padding."

"They are a very proud guild, I believe."

"He told me one thing that shocked me a good deal. For years I have been worrying myself sick, wondering why yaks' tails were imported into the United States from Tibet. I could not understand there being any popular demand for them. I know that if someone came up to me and said 'Mr. Wodehouse, I have long been a great admirer of your work and would like to make some small return for the many happy hours you have given me. Take this yak's tail, and make of it a constant companion,' I would thank him and giggle a little and say how frightfully good of him and it was just what I had been wanting, but I should most certainly leave the thing in the subway on my way home. I now have the facts. Yaks' tails are used for making beards for department-store Santa Clauses. You wince, I notice."

"Yes, I do. I find a picture rising before my eyes of some unfortunate yak wandering around Tibet without a tail.

You don't have to know much about the sensitive nature of the yak to realize what this must mean."

"It bathes the bereaved animal in confusion?"

"He doesn't know which way to look. But enough of a distasteful subject. Tell me more about these changes that you have observed. In what other respect does the New York of 1956 differ from the New York of 1904?"

"One notices an extraordinary improvement in the manners of the populace."

"You find them polished these days?"

"They are all as polite as pallbearers. It may be Emily Post's daily advice on deportment that has brought about the change. Or perhaps it is because I have been over here, setting them a good example."

"Possibly."

"Probably. When I first came to the country, New Yorkers were all splendid fellows, but inclined to be a little on the brusque side. They snarled at you. They shoved you and asked curtly who you were shoving. At baseball games it was customary to advocate the assassination of the um-

pire and to start the good work off by hurling pop bottles at him. One of my earliest recollections of the city is of watching a mob of travelers trying to enter a subway train and getting jammed in the doorway. Two subway officials were standing on the platform, and the first subway official said to the second subway official, 'Pile 'em in, George, pile 'em in.' Whereupon the two put their heads down and took a running dive at the mass like members of a football team bucking the line. It was effective, it was as though those passengers had been shot out of a gun, but it could not happen today."

"I get what you mean. George and his colleague would at least say 'Pardon us, gentlemen.' "

"Exactly. You see it everywhere, this new courtesy. Billy Rose recalls the occasion when he was driving his car and stalled the engine at a street intersection. The lights changed from green to red and from red back to green again, but Billy continued to maintain his status quo. A policeman came over. 'What's the matter, son?' he asked sympathetically. 'Haven't we any colors you like?' "

"He could scarcely have been nicer, could he?"

"Boxers, too, not so long ago a somewhat uncouth section of the community who were seldom if ever mistaken for members of the Vere de Vere family, have now a polish which makes their society a pleasure. There was a boxer at the St. Nicholas Rink not long ago who came up against an antagonist with a disagreeably forceful left hook which he kept applying to the jaw and the lower ribs. The victim's manager watched pallidly from outside the ropes, and when his tiger came back to his corner at the end of the round he was all concern and compassion.

" 'Joey,' he asked anxiously, 'how do you feel?'

" 'Fine, thank you,' said the boxer. 'And you?' One can almost hear Emily Post cheering in the background."

"Quite."

"Even the criminal classes have caught the spirit. From Passaic, New Jersey, comes the news that an unidentified assailant plunged a knife into the shoulder of James F. Dobson, spun him around and then, seeing his face, uttered a sharp exclamation. 'Oh, I beg your pardon,' he said. 'I got the wrong guy.'

"Frank and manly. It was what Emily Post has always insisted on. If you find yourself in the wrong, admit it and apologize."

"What you say is very gratifying, Mr. Wodehouse. Then America is all right, you think?"

"With one grave exception. I allude to the matter of divorce."

"Too much of it, you feel?"

"Too little, my good sir. It's heartbreaking. When Australia regained the Davis Cup, there was not unnaturally chagrin and disappointment and a tendency on the part of the citizenry to let the upper lip unstiffen a bit, but the downhearted were able to console themselves with the reflection that, whatever might happen on the tennis court, in one field America still led the world. Her supremacy in the matter of divorce remained unchallenged. Patriots pointed with pride at the figures, which showed that while thirteen—I think it was thirteen—in every thousand American ever-loving couples decided each year to call it a day, the best the nearest competitor, Switzerland, could do was three. 'As long as we have Arline Judge, Hollywood film stars and Tommy Manville,' people told one another, 'we're all right. Come the three corners of the world in arms, and we shall shock them.' And, of course, at times they did, considerably.

"But now there has been a rude awakening. We learn from the New York *Daily Mirror* that 'an amazing thing has been happening, little noticed, in our national life. Since 1946 there has been a forty-per-cent decline in the number of divorces.' Just like that. No preparation, no leading up to it, no attempt to break the thing gently. It is as if the *Mirror* had crept up behind America and struck her on the back of the head with a sock full of wet sand.

"The paper omits to mention what is happening in Switzerland, but one assumes that the Swiss are still plugging along in the old dogged way and maybe by this time have got up to five or even six per thousand. For don't run away with the idea that the Swiss do nothing but yodel and make milk chocolate. They have plenty of leisure, be well assured, for divorce actions. Probably at this very moment some citizen of the inland republic is on the witness stand showing the judge the lump on his head where the little woman hit him with a cuckoo clock."

"And where do you place the blame?"

"Certainly not on Hollywood. The spirit of the men there is splendid. Every day one reads in the gossip columns another of those heart-warming announcements to the effect that Lotta Svelte and George Marsupial are holding hands and plan to merge as soon as the former can disentangle herself from Marcus Manleigh and the latter from Belinda Button, and one knows that George and Lotta are not going to let the side down. In due season she will be in court telling the judge that for a week the marriage was a very happy one, but then George started reading the paper at breakfast and refusing to listen when she told him of the dream she had had last night, thus causing her deep mental distress. No, the heart of Hollywood is sound."

"It may be that it is the judges who are lacking in team spirit. A great deal must always depend on the judges."

"Some of them are all right. Not a word of complaint about the one in Hackensack, who recently granted Mrs. Carmella Porretta a divorce because her husband, Salvatore, struck her with a buttered muffin. We applaud also his learned brother in Indianapolis who allowed Mrs. Dorothy Whitehouse to sever the knot because her husband, Donald, insisted on buying the groceries and always brought home ham, to which she was allergic. But what are we to say of Domestic Relations Judge Richard Douglass of Knoxville, who, when Mrs. Edna Hunt Tankersley applied to him for her twelfth divorce, callously informed her that as far as he was concerned she had got her 'final final decree'? In other words, when this devoted woman, all eagerness to see America first, comes up for the thirteenth time, her industry and determination will be unrewarded. No baker's dozen for Edna, unless, of course, she is shrewd enough to take her custom elsewhere.

"Has Judge Douglass never reflected that it is just this sort of thing that discourages ambition and is going to hand the world's leadership to the Swiss on a plate with watercress round it?

"Nor are all the states pulling their weight. Some are above reproach. In Washington, for instance, there are eleven separate and distinct grounds for divorce. But in South Carolina divorce is actually not permitted. Can one be surprised that the Swiss, who pull together as one man in every patriotic movement, are steadily creeping up and likely to forge ahead at any moment?"

"Of course, we may be in just a temporary slump. You know how these strange lapses from form happen from time to time. Willie Mays couldn't hit a thing at the beginning of last season. Maybe we have become overconfident. Or do you think that the modern American husband, instead of getting a divorce, finds it cheaper to dissect his bride with the meat axe and deposit the debris in a sack in the back yard?"

"I doubt it. One has heard, of course, of the man in Chicago named Young who once, when his nerves were unstrung, put his wife, Josephine, in the chopping machine and canned her and labeled her 'Tongue,' but as a rule the American wife does not murder easy."

"You have some special case in mind?"

"I was thinking of the young husband and wife in California. For three or four days, it seems, theirs was a happy marriage, but then, and as so often happens, the husband became restless and anxious for a change. At first he thought of divorce, and then he thought again and remembered the Californian community law which gives the sundered wife half her husband's property. And he was just reconciling himself to putting a new coat of paint on her and trying to make her do for another year, when an idea struck him. Why not say it with rattlesnakes?"

"Odd how one has these inspirations."

"So he got a rattlesnake and put it in the pocket of his trousers and hung the trousers over a chair in the bedroom, and when his wife asked him for some money, he told her she would find his wallet in his trousers pocket.

" 'In the bedroom,' he said, and she went into the bedroom, whence her voice presently emerged.

" 'Which trousers?'

" 'The gray ones.'

" 'The ones hanging on the chair?'

" 'That's right.'

" 'Which pocket?'

" 'The hip pocket.'

" 'But I've looked there,' said his wife discontentedly, 'and all I could find was a rattlesnake.'

2

"So you see it is not so simple."

"Still, if we all pull shoulder to shoulder . . . What is needed is something in the nature of a crusade."

"I intend to start one."

"Ah, yes, you have recently become an American citizen, have you not?"

"I have, and a red-blooded one, at that. I had always been a sort of honorary American, but it seemed to me that the time had come when I ought to start running things. There will be a lot of changes around here, now I've got the vote. I shall take a firm line with juvenile delinquency, for instance. It is getting so nowadays that you can't go for a stroll without having some teen-ager hold you up with a gun and stick lighted matches between your toes. I shall vote against this."

"What are your views on referendum and the initiative?"

"Yes."

"And housing conditions?"

"I am in favor of them."

"Will you vote Democrat or Republican?"

"Probably."

"Thank you, Mr. Wodehouse."